The Five Approaches to Acting Series

BUILDING IMAGES

WRITTEN BY DAVID KAPLAN

Hansen Publishing Group, LLC
East Brunswick, New Jersey
www.hansenpublishing.com

The Five Approaches to Acting Series: Building Images
Copyright © 2007 David Kaplan

Trademarks

Warning and Disclaimer

International Standard Book Number: 978-1-60182-183-6

Hansen Publishing Group, LLC
302 Ryders Lane
East Brunswick, New Jersey
732-220-1211
www.hansenpublishing.com

The Publisher gratefully acknowledges the copyright holders who have agreed to have their works excerpted here. The next page constitutes a continuation of this copyright page.

Excerpts from THE ODD COUPLE copyright © 1966 by Neil Simon, copyright renewed 1994 by Neil Simon. Professionals and amateurs are hereby warned that THE ODD COUPLE is fully protected under the United States Copyright Act, the Berne Convention, and the Universal Copyright Convention and is subject to royalty. All rights, including without limitation professional, amateur, motion picture, television, radio, recitation, lecturing, public reading and foreign translation rights, computer media rights and the right of reproduction, and electronic storage or retrieval, in whole or in part and in any form, are strictly reserved and none of these rights can be exercised or used without written permission from the copyright owner. Inquiries for stock and amateur performances should be addressed to Samuel French, Inc., 45 West 25th Street, New York, NY 10010. All other inquiries should be addressed to Gary N. DaSilva, 111 N. Sepulveda Blvd., Suite 250, Manhattan Beach, CA 90266-6850.
    Excerpts from THE LEARNED LADIES (THE SCHOOL FOR WIVES) by Jean-Baptiste Poquelin de Molière, English translation copyright © 1978, 1977 by Richard Wilbur, copyright © 1978 by Harcourt, Inc., reprinted by permission of the publisher. CAUTION: Professionals and amateurs are hereby warned that THE LEARNED LADIES is subject to a royalty. It is fully protected under the copyright laws of the United States of America, and of all countries covered by the International Copyright Union (including the Dominion of Canada and the rest of the British Commonwealth), and of all countries covered by the Universal Copyright Convention and the Pan-American Copyright Convention, and of all countries with which the United States has reciprocal copyright relations. All rights, including professional, amateur, motion picture, recitation, lecturing, public reading, radio broadcasting, television and the rights of translation into foreign languages, are strictly reserved. Particular emphasis is laid on the question of readings, permission for which must be secured from the author's agent in writing. All inquiries (except for amateur rights) should be addressed to Gilbert Parker, Curtis Brown Ltd., 575 Madison Avenue, New York NY 10022. The amateur acting rights of THE LEARNED LADIES are controlled exclusively by the Dramatists Play Service, Inc., 440 Park Avenue South, New York, NY 10016. No amateur performances of the play may be given without obtaining in advance the written permission of the Dramatists Play Service Inc., and paying the requisite fee.
    Excerpts from THE LESSON and THE BALD SOPRANO from *The Bald Soprano and Other Plays* by Eugene Ionesco, translated by Donald M. Allen, © 1958 by Grove Press Inc., used by permission of Grove/Atlantic, Inc.

CREDITS

To Edwin W. Schloss,

Prince of friends, open-hearted, open-eyed.

CONTENTS

SCRIPT ANALYSIS COMPARATIVE REFERENCE CHART

	TASK/ACTION ANALYSIS	EPISODIC ANALYSIS	BUILDING IMAGES ANALYSIS	WORLD OF THE PLAY ANALYSIS	NARRATIVE ANALYSIS
BASIC UNIT	Task	Episode	Image	Social context; behavior and form	Event Point of view
ILLUSION OF CHARACTER	Web of relationships	Playing the opposition	String of masks	Distinctions within the context of the world	Intersection of point of view and events
DRAMATIC ACTION	Action meeting an obstacle	Transaction or *gest*	Moment when mask changes	Breach in the rules of the world	Shifting the point of view
KEY QUESTION	What do I need to do?	What do I do? What is my role?	What is this like? What does this make me think of?	What are the values of the world?	What am I describing? What is my point of view?
UNIFYING IMAGE	Oil painting	Poster	Collage	Frame	Film camera angles
RELATIVE THEORY	Freud Psychoanalysis	Alfred Adler Transactional analysis Marxism	Carl Jung Personae	Ruth Benedict Cultural anthropology	Derrida Literary deconstructionism
SUITABLE PLAYWRIGHTS	Chekhov Ibsen Strindberg	Shakespeare Brecht Ionesco	Strindberg Lorca Genet Williams	Molière Wilde O'Neill Beckett	Shakespeare the Greeks Williams Shepard
AUDIENCE	Compassionate	Judgmental	Passionate	Transported	Participatory

PART III

BUILDING IMAGES

Reading List
The Maids by Jean Genet
Yerma by Federico García Lorca
Stanislavsky in Focus (chapters 2 and 6) by Sharon Marie Carnicke

Viewing List
Dinner at Eight directed by George Cukor
Touch of Evil directed by Orson Welles

Max Ernst, detail from *Quietude*

CHAPTER 1

Masks

Olivier's Nose and Your Mother's Hat

Laurence Olivier had the good luck to be born into a time and place that recognized his talent and offered opportunities to apply it. In 1916, at the age of ten, he played Brutus in a school production in London, a startling performance that happened to be attended by the celebrated actress Ellen Terry. She wrote in her diary: "The small boy who played Brutus is already a great actor" (49). In 1972, at seventy-eight, Olivier played King Lear (on television). With nearly ninety-eight stage productions in between, he is widely admired as one of the greatest actors of his or any generation.

It was sometimes Olivier's practice to begin work on his most difficult roles by changing the shape of his nose. He also liked to rig himself out with wigs, false teeth, and putty for his forehead and chin. More than once he began the job by disguising his voice. Olivier's Othello spoke almost a full octave lower than the actor's natural pitch, an effect he worked at for several months before rehearsals began. He used what appealed to him. For the role of Richard III, Olivier based his characterization, in part, on the Big Bad Wolf from the Disney cartoon version of *Little Red Riding Hood*.

"I'm afraid I do work mostly from the outside in," Olivier said in response to an interviewer asking about his craft. He went on to say, "Perhaps I should mention what everybody's been talking about for years, and that's the Actors Studio and the Method. What I've just said is absolutely against their beliefs, absolute heresy" (50).

Olivier's heresy is any actor's healthy instinct, a child's pleasure in pretending to be someone else by putting on mother's hat. Mother's hat or rubber nose, it's playful to assume another person's character. That's why, in English, we speak about acting in a *play*, not a *depression*. The necessary prop for the game of pretending to be someone else is a mask, and although they don't cover the whole face, your mother's hat and Olivier's fake nose are both masks. In addition to his *visual mask*, Olivier's lowered pitch as Othello was a *vocal mask*. Changing the sound of his own voice helped to transform the British actor into a Moorish general as effectively as, if not more than, his three layers of black make-up.

Masks make appealing toys for children—and for actors—by offering the possibility of acting out fantasies safely and playfully. The camouflage of a mask gives you permission to shout, to rage, to love indiscriminately, to break rules without fear of punishment, or to obey rules you wouldn't ordinarily care about. A mask puts you at a distance from your actions; it is the character—not you—who rages, who flirts, who kills. The joy in this is so strong that many cultures have occasions, like Mardi Gras, when ordinarily sober people may safely act out flamboyant behavior they would never consider at any other time—once they slip on a mask.

For a professional actor, masks make powerful tools that do more than masquerade. The mask also serves to unleash hidden personality traits. Look at Olivier's nose. He couldn't. Although the actor couldn't see his own nose onstage, it nonetheless had as potent an effect on him as it did on the audience. For any actor who chooses to do so, an outer mask may evoke a yet more play-sustaining *inner mask*.

Inner masks, which we'll call *images*, have the power to transform an actor as effectively as any disguise. Some actors skip the outer masks entirely by the time they get to performance—including wigs and costume changes—and base their transformation to another person on an inner foundation. Eleonora Duse, for example, performed without make-up. Her ability to transform her height, her age, and her appearance derived from inner images, described by more than one observer as an inner flame. From 1905 to 1956, the American solo artist Ruth Draper performed without scenery, but with sufficient conviction to persuade her audiences that they were witnessing a crowded church when there was nothing onstage but the actress, curtains, and a plain chair. Draper herself needed little more than a shawl or a hat to transform from one character to another. The tradition endures. The American actress Anna Deveare Smith has played Hasidic Jews, African-American politicians, and Korean grocers with little more than a switch of her hat.

In an effort to sweep clichés from the stage, 1950s partisans of what was understood to be the Stanislavsky System (following the interpretation called "The Method," discussed in Chapter 3) were proud to exclude external masks, which they called "working from the outside in," not just during performances but at rehearsal, too. The orthodox way for a Method actor to work was to get in touch with the deep-felt memories of personal experience. From that point of view, Olivier's claim to "heresy" was true.

Of course, the alleged heresy of an external choice is just another road to inner reality. Look at the example of Sarah Bernhardt, an actress accused of so divorcing inner from outer images that it was said she could play a death scene with one hand sticking out from behind a screen and, with her other hand unseen by the weeping audience, wave hello to a friend in the wings. Sarah Bernhardt was, in some ways, the successor to the great Rachel, who had died young of consumption. Bernhardt was Jewish too, or at least her mother was a Jew, which for most Jews is what counts. As for her father, better you shouldn't ask. When it came to actresses, at least, the French were interested in classical poses, not bloodlines.

Bernhardt could stand and recite with the best of them, in a voice described as molten gold. Her body was unusually thin. She was teased about her thinness as a girl and ridiculed for it as a woman—until her own fame made being slim fashionable. Onstage, her fragility contrasted well with the volcanic energy she displayed. She had the good taste to include some stately classical gestures, but she also could—and would—abandon herself to the moment and writhe, twist, and swoon, her golden voice swooping from croak to croon. Bernhardt's technique was spine-tingling. Contemporaries compared her showmanship to Duse's realism, with a full understanding that these were rival ideas of what was great art.

Yet Bernhardt's devices were not meant to simply dazzle the audience—they were meant to dazzle Bernhardt. When she was asked why she painted henna on the palms of her hands as Cleopatra—a detail the audience would never notice—she said she did it so that if she looked at her own hands, they would be those of the Queen of Egypt. At sixty-five, with a wooden leg, Bernhardt would play the teen-age Joan of Arc* and audiences found her convincing (51). What difference did it make how old she really was? The performance of the gestures and the timbre of the voice created the illusion of character onstage, but more importantly, they convinced the lady herself that, in her own mind, she was a young girl again.

Ruth Draper once asked Eleonora Duse if Duse knew how she made herself seem larger or taller, depending on the role, something Draper herself could do without knowing how she did it. Duse laughed. Duse had asked Bernhardt, who had told her to ask Draper.† For all their differences in personal style—Draper alone onstage, Duse seemingly bare of technique, Bernhardt smothered in grandiosity—all three of them relied on the same source to power their performances: *personal inner images*.

Literary critics speak of images when they look at how words of the text set up patterns, like musical motifs. In *Macbeth*, for example, when the text mentions *clothes*, the clothes are uncomfortable. This discomfort points a clever actor to an understanding of Macbeth's guilt. (This kind of text analysis is very useful for a performer, and we will talk about it at length in Part IV: *Inhabiting the World of the Play*.) Still, an actor's use of a play is *personal*, and actors working with images must do something literary critics need not: clarify the meaning of the text by relating the words to themselves.

For now, when we refer to *imagery analysis* we are talking about an actor's internal set of images, and how an actor's idiosyncratic and personal set of images can be united with a script to yield results of great power and emotional truth. When it works, it makes for electric performances. Performers who use such images act as creative as well as interpretive artists. They arrive at rehearsals with their own sets of ideas, that is to say, the masks, external and internal, which move them to *play* in both senses of the word: as children and as mature professionals.

Ignore the playwright's images—for now

This part of the book is about the ways actors might first build their own personal images and then apply them to embody the images of the playwright and the play. Why ignore the playwright's images in order to return to them? Simply put, they are the playwright's images, not yours—at least not yet. It does happen, of course, that the words of the text will prod direct responses from your gut. If you are a lucky actor, you'll get the roles you are born to play; in preparation and performance your personal content

---

*The play was Emile Moreau's *Procès de Jeanne d'Arc*.

†Draper met other theater greats that month she was in Paris. In her diary, she noted that she had had a nice talk with Stanislavsky and that he was a wonderful man.

will be very rich. Interestingly, this does not necessarily happen when your life experience parallels your character's. Such a close resemblance can paralyze a performer instead of bestowing the detachment and freedom that a mask offers.

The playwright's words have the power to paralyze a performer in other ways. The beauty and complexity of the play's imagery will sometimes intimidate you so much that your own understanding seems insignificant and the play unapproachable. And, yes, there are times when you will not be moved by the playwright's images, or, if you are moved by evocative words on the page, you will often not have had the life experience (say, killing yourself, if you're playing a suicide) to grasp the playwright's ideas or the character's feelings.

In such situations, you want to try to use an image of your own to give content to what you are saying. Although Lillian Gish summarized her training as speaking so everyone could hear her, if you are going to ask twelve or twelve hundred strangers to sit in the dark and listen to you recite, perhaps you had better bring more than a loud voice to your role. You might bring something to say about the text. Better still, you might find ways the text is meaningful to you and your life, too, or the management will find someone else for whom it is meaningful. Without personal content, performances are essentially inhuman, even when they are technically proficient.

The Rosetta Stone and Images of the Play

The words of a play you do not understand, no matter how beautiful or profound, resemble rows of unreadable hieroglyphics. They will stay unreadable until you carve yourself a personal *Rosetta Stone*. What's the Rosetta Stone? In 1799, French archeologists accompanying Napoleon's Egyptian Expedition to the Rosetta arm of the Nile discovered a slab of granite inscribed with writing in two languages, Ancient Greek and Egyptian hieroglyphics. Ancient Greek was still read in Napoleon's France, thanks to monks and librarians who preserved and translated classical texts. The ability to understand Egyptian hieroglyphics, however, was long forgotten.

This stone with the same information in two languages became a key to reading hieroglyphics once the decipherers compared the hieroglyphics to the Greek. How did they know the text was the same in Greek and hieroglyphics? Because the few words they did recognize were famous names—among them, Cleopatra's*—and these names were repeated in the same place in both texts.

The process is the same for you as a performer using your own images—the language you know—to decipher the images of the play. Out in the desert of rehearsal, whipped by the hot winds of scorn, you'll be digging up your own Rosetta Stone to unearth your own key to translate the hieroglyphics of the script. Remember that no matter how beautiful the playwright's hieroglyphics might be, if you can't understand them,

---

*Not Bernhardt's or Liz Taylor's Cleopatra, but an ancestor of the Serpent of the Nile who lived 150 years earlier, in 196 BCE. A few other words that could be recognized on the Rosetta Stone in both languages were *temples*, *Greeks*, and the word for *him* (third person masculine pronoun). Hmmm.

neither will the audience. At first, you may make contact with only a few places—like Cleopatra's name—but eventually you will begin to translate more and more of the play.

Strindberg's Dreams

To prepare ways to use your own images in the theater, it's inspiring to learn about the playwrights for whom imagery—rather than plot or character—is at the heart of a play. At the same time that Chekhov and Ibsen were challenging nineteenth-century story-dominated melodrama with character-dominated realism, the Swedish writer August Strindberg was creating dramatic texts dominated by images. Strindberg was part of the movement toward greater realism in the theater, yet his idea of what was real was not a common one. He was convinced of the existence of vampires. He was certain that women were in a conspiracy to steal power from men. He believed that the world glowed from within with psychic energy. Ibsen kept a picture of Strindberg over his desk, and referred to the fiery-eyed Swede in the portrait as *that madman*. Strindberg did in fact spend time in a sanitarium. More than once in his life he was willing to travel across the borders of insanity in order to retrieve a vision. August Strindberg was, at times, willfully mad, just as Brecht willfully stank.

The attempt to explain human behavior as a logical mechanism, a task that fascinated actors like Stanislavsky, psychologists like Freud, novelists like Zola, and playwrights like Brecht, held no such fascination for Strindberg. Neither poses nor motivated behavior could fully satisfy the requirements of a Strindberg play like *The Ghost Sonata*, *To Damascus*, or *A Dream Play* (in which dead men walk, a castle melts into a chrysanthemum, and goddesses descend from heaven). Strindberg stated the method to his madness in his Author's Note to *A Dream Play* (52), written in 1901:

> In this dream play, the author has . . . attempted to imitate the inconsequent yet transparently logical shape of a dream. Everything can happen, everything is possible and probable. Time and place do not exist; on an insignificant basis of reality, the imagination spins, weaving new patterns; a mixture of memories, experiences, free fancies, incongruities and improvisations. The characters split, double, multiply, evaporate, condense, disperse, assemble.

That's an excellent description of the process of an actor building images of a role; any role, not just those in dream plays. You'll notice when you rehearse with images that they do not advance logically, methodically, or deliberately. In rehearsal and in performance, inner masks do indeed split, double, multiply, evaporate, condense, disperse, and assemble—just as Strindberg described.

As you build a collection of images, an illusion of character is created that is as convincing as any created by pursuing a task or playing a role in an episode. Often, creating a role by building images is a faster and bolder process than running actions into obstacles or haggling over transactions. This dynamic idea—*identity as a shifting collec-*

tion of images—echoes a theory of psychology developed by a Freudian heretic, the Swiss-born psychologist Carl Jung.

Carl Jung and Mythology

Carl Jung began as Freud's distinguished disciple, just as Meyerhold began as Stanislavsky's protégé. Jung was nineteen years younger than Freud, the older man's hope for the future in the new science of psychology. Yet, just as Meyerhold diverted the course of Stanislavsky's revolution by offering another approach to acting besides identifying needs and taking actions onstage to satisfy them, Jung offered another explanation for behavior besides Freud's identification of desire.

What Freud called Jung's "betrayal" happened by 1912, after Freud had established psychology as a discipline and had refined his definition of human motivation as the collision of desire and present circumstances. We've already discussed how those ideas parallel Stanislavsky's insistence on an actor having a task in a performance, where actions encounter obstacles. What Jung noticed and thought important—an insight later corroborated by many other psychologists—is that sometimes people behave in certain ways because, consciously or not, they are acting out an image, rather than fulfilling a desire. These images fill a pattern in a story so deeply-believed that the story can be called a *personal myth*. When adolescents, for example, smoke and drink to excess, it's because they are acting out a myth of *rebellion*. Weak people become strong under pressure because they are acting out an inner image of *strength and power*. Jung observed the same wars that Brecht observed and concluded that soldiers run off to be killed not for any logical reason, but because they are acting out a myth of *chivalry and patriotism*. Jung claimed that identifying a person's mythology of internal images explained human behavior and identity just as thoroughly as, and perhaps more than, analyzing a person's motivation, desire, or toilet training.

To take an example from a play, Hedda Gabler is a general's daughter. She issues orders to her husband as if he were a soldier; when her life defeats her she shoots herself dead using the general's pistol, the way a warrior who has lost a war might kill himself. Hedda has a man's self-assurance in a world of deferential women because her *image* of herself is *masculine*.

Jung's theories apply to the work of an actor because, for Jung, images are not isolated or self-sufficient, they are entire systems of relationships, to other people and to the world. Hedda's mythic role as General's Daughter casts Løvborg as her Incompetent Captain, and her husband as a Naïve Civilian. In real life, when people fantasize that they are persecuted, they assign other people the role of Persecutors. An actor who reinterprets the roles and events of the play according to an image is reproducing that process.

Archetypes and personae

Jung observed that people wear different masks in different situations: we are children in the presence of our parents, we are parents in the presence of our children. As people make their way through their lives they acquire new and different masks, from apprentice to master, from virgin to bride. Onstage or off, these collections of masks are what we call "character."

- Woman, Temptress, Harlot's daughter, Mother, Actress, Eccentric, Romantic, Ugly Little Girl . . . *voila*: Sarah Bernhardt!
- Woman, Wife, Actress, Agitator, Survivor, Refugee, Technician, Head Wife Among Many . . . *ach so*: Helene Weigel!
- General's Daughter, Bored Wife, Romantic Lover, Town Beauty, Newlywed, Tortured Soul . . . *ja ja*: Hedda Gabler!
- Insightful Doctor, Stern Prophet, Noble Father, Trouble-making Jew . . . *oy vey*: Sigmund Freud!

When an actor creates a role by building images, he reproduces the way people collect images for "acting out" the roles of their life. Some of these roles are universal, which Jung called *archetypes* (*Woman, Wife*), some are cultural (*General's Daughter, Trouble-making Jew*), some are historical (*Romantic, Refugee*), some are professional (*Actress, Harlot*), some are personal (*Ugly Little Girl*—which was all too clearly a personal image of Bernhardt's—and *Head Wife*—who knows what Helene Weigel really thought of Brecht's philandering?). Each of us is a collection of masks, which Jung called *personae*, carved for us and by us as a result of our life experiences. The word *persona* is Latin for an "actor's mask."

Jung believed that these images were gateways to what he called the *collective unconscious*. In their own particular way, your myths and personal history echo everyone else's myths. The content of a *mother archetype* will remain the same as long as there are people, even if the form of the archetype is culturally and personally determined. Your Chinese mother urging you to eat rice is also an Italian mother passing the pasta and, yes, a Jewish mother pushing the chicken soup, because it's the same the whole world over: for mothers, Food is Love.

As an actor, you play from your own images knowing that you will connect to the archetypes of the audience. You can stuff yourself with ravioli, content that the Beijing audience watching you is relating to their own experience with wontons.

The String of Masks

The rehearsal process using images can be thought of as carving yourself a **string of masks**. You can do this by creating an outer mask (Olivier's nose) or an inner mask (Duse's flame). Either way can lead to the other and to the audience. Even the most personal and private images have the power to communicate with an audience when those images are heartfelt. Members of the audience can tell when an actor crosses a bridge to the subconscious world, and they can be persuaded, by the actor's example, to cross over on their own—to the collective unconscious. Just as the audience is meant to be sympathetic watching a performance structured by tasks, or prodded to judgment by the presentation of oppositions, an audience in the presence of deeply felt images is meant to become impassioned. Even a performer's most personal and private images can move an audience—if they are images that move the performer.

A strong image resonates with an audience, but does not necessarily echo or reconstruct itself in their hearts and minds. For example, if you care passionately about beans, it is your passion the audience will respond to, not necessarily split peas and lentils. Audience members will not always share the same image, nor should they. They will relate your passion to passions of their own.

There is a passage from Balzac's novel *Father Goriot* (1834) that gives an illustration of the power of images. An ambitious young man is listening to a father explain why he lives like a beggar so that his daughters may live like princesses:

> There was something sublime about Father Goriot; Eugene had never, till now, seen him aflame with love for his daughters. It is worthy of remark that true feeling acts like an inspiration. No matter how ordinary a man may be, whenever he gives expression to a real and strong affection, he is wrapped in an impalpable essence that alters his countenance, animates his gestures and lends a new inflection to his voice. Under the stress of passion, the dullest being may reach the highest degree of eloquence of thought, if not of language, and seems to be transfigured. At this moment, the old man's voice and gestures possessed the communicative power that marks a great actor. Are not our fine feelings the poetry of the will? (53).

"The poetry of the will" calls for performers to play with images the way poets play with words. In life, our masks are built up through experience; onstage, our images are built up in rehearsals.

Terms to Work with: Images

Image

Imagery analysis has a single term to agree on, and it's an easy one to remember: an **image**. Using this approach, the word *image* refers to a private idea you are reminded of by the script, character, line, or moment. An image is not always a picture; it can be a sound, a smell, a touch, a memory, a taste. The word itself is derived from the Latin *imago*, a root that reveals a relationship between the words *imitation*, *imagination*, and, perhaps, *magic*. For actors, an image is written as a simile. It answers the questions:

- What does this resemble?
- What is this like?
- What does this remind me of?

MASKS

Some examples from scenes we've discussed so far:

- Richard III is as smooth as new suede when he makes love to Anne.
- Natalya Petrovna is as charming as the song of a bird.
- Ionesco's Professor reminds you of the sour smell of your childhood piano teacher.
- Ionesco's Pupil reminds you of the time you flunked spelling in sixth grade.
- Hedda Gabler is like a caged wolf.
- Shlink is as bitter as the sound of his name.

Images can be divided into two kinds: *fantasy* and *personal history*.

Fantasy

A **fantasy** is just that: anything you can imagine yourself being and—like the little child dressing up in Mother's hat—would like to act out. For example: animals, rock stars, super-heroes, royalty, clowns, criminals, soldiers, thieves, Hedda Gabler as a caged wolf, or Hedda Gabler as Tina Turner, or Hedda Gabler as you imagine Ibsen to have imagined her. Acting out fantasies is at the heart of an actor's experience onstage, from Olivier's nose to Anna Deveare Smith's Korean grocer.

When Stella Adler diverged from the teachings of then-accepted American understanding of Stanislavsky, it was in order to harness the instinct toward fantasy and take to heart Stanislavsky's phrase *"what if?"*: "What if I were a wolf? What if I were a general's daughter?" The impulse was kept reined to the structure of tasks by the next question: "Well, if I were a wolf—what would I do?" In class, Adler urged her students to do more than investigate their own lives; she would, for example, teach whole classes in how to behave like royalty. Her most succinct comment on the subject: "Your life is one millionth of what you know. Your talent is your imagination. The rest is lice" (54).

Personal history

Memories of your life's experiences make up the images of **personal history**. When the Professor of *The Lesson* reminds you of the smell of your piano teacher, or the events of the play lead you to remember the time in sixth grade when you flunked spelling, these are the images of personal history. Lee Strasberg urged actors to draw on personal history to identify and put into use what were called *affective memories*, a term derived from the writings of Stanislavsky and borrowed from the now-outdated experiments of the French psychologist Théodule Ribot. The theory of affective memories is that events from the past settle into the mind and body and remain capable of being accessed. It is not, as has often been assumed or taught, that an affective memory is relived. It is *remembered*, and, as a result, *emotional memories* arise that an actor can learn to access and put to use.

Sometimes personal history and emotional memory diverge. An emotional memory may change over time as the person remembering ages and gains perspective on the original experience. The theory is that emotional memories provide a lodestone of truth by returning you, like a compass pointing north, to the basic truth of your personal history. Echoing the *beads/bits/beats* brouhaha, Shelley Winters said in an interview that she always thought Strasberg was saying "effective memories" because they were always so effective (55).

Which is better—history or fantasy?

Answering this question is the basis for bitter and unending arguments. When Lee Strasberg died in 1982, news reached Stella Adler while she was in class. She asked her students to pause for a minute to pay respect. She looked at her watch as the minute ticked by. At the end of the last second she burst out, "That man has done more to ruin the American theater than anyone else."*

Emotional memories derived from your own personal history are undeniably potent. What could be more personal than what you experience first-hand in your own life? But as any psychologist or thinking adult knows, memories are *not* facts or experiences. Memories collect experience. When a net is dipped into the sea, as fine as the mesh might be, the water and a few fish will still slip away. To some degree, then, so-called "history" is *already* fantasy.

It works the other way, too, since fantasy is reality based. Our imaginations recombine experience. The mixture might be something new, but the fantasy is always an aspect of personal history. Freud famously said you are all the people in your dreams; you are certainly all the people in your fantasies.

The answer to the question of which source is better for an actor's image—fantasy or personal history—is that neither is better. Both are aspects of the same collision of experience and interpretation. Because fantasy buffers the difficulties and pain of memory, most people find it easier to start with a fantasy. If you can relate more directly to your own life, begin there. "I never travel without my diary," says Gwendolyn in Oscar Wilde's *The Importance of Being Earnest* (1899). "One should always have something sensational to read on the train."

Fantasy or personal history, the challenge is exactly the same: to translate the actor's images to the specifics of the text. When this task remains undone, criticism of images as self-indulgent and diversionary from the job of acting the play is valid. In this chapter we will explore a script using fantasy; in the next chapter we will simulate the experience of emotional memories based on personal history.

Assembling Images: Rehearsing a Scene from *The Maids*

Let's explore an actor's personal imagery rehearsing a scene from Jean Genet's 1947 play, *The Maids* (56). We're going to talk a lot more openly about images than you would ever want to in rehearsal. Images, by definition, are private and thrive on discretion.

---

*Musical theater mentor David Craig would relate this anecdote in his classes. His students now repeat it to their students.

Words can oversimplify such a complex mixture of ideas, impressions, desires, and dreams. In this way, images resemble emotions, which are also private and hard to describe or pin down with words. Yet there are techniques for an actor to structure emotions, just as there are techniques for structuring images.

First, a few notes about the play. In *The Maids*, two servants—Solange and Claire—rehearse the ritual murder of their mistress. The servants, who are sisters, take turns playing murderer or victim. The victim always masquerades as the mistress of the house, imitating Madame's affectations while wearing Madame's discarded wigs and soiled gowns. The sister performing the murderer masquerades as the younger maid, Claire. Sometimes it really is Claire, sometimes "Claire" is the older sister, Solange. But in the ritual murder, it is invariably "Claire" who kills "Madame."

One night, the rehearsals of the ritual murder conclude. The sisters attempt the genuine murder and poison Madame's tea. Despite her servants' polite insistence, Madame avoids even a sip before she gaily departs for a romantic rendezvous. We'll begin with Madame's entrance, which is midway through this one-act play.

> *A burst of nervous laughter backstage.* MADAME, *in a fur coat, enters laughing with* SOLANGE *behind her.*

MADAME There's no end to it! Such horrible gladioli, such a sickly pink, and mimosa! They probably hunt through the market before dawn to get them cheaper. (SOLANGE *helps her off with her coat*)

SOLANGE Madame wasn't too cold?

MADAME Yes, Solange, I was very cold. I've been trailing through corridors all night long. I've been seeing frozen men and stony faces, but I did manage to catch a glimpse of Monsieur. From a distance. I waved to him. I've only just left the wife of a magistrate. Claire!

SOLANGE She's preparing Madame's tea.

MADAME I wish she'd hurry. I'm ashamed to ask for tea when Monsieur is all alone, without a thing, without food, without cigarettes.

Embrace the arbitrary

If nothing comes to mind at first, don't worry, it will. Wait. It will. Images erupt spontaneously, without poking. Sooner or later the script will remind you of something. When an image comes to you, don't question if it's the best image—or hunt for its source—embrace it for being random. Whether it's a fantasy or a personal experience, either is fine. Don't derail yourself searching for real life equivalents for fantasies or a "better" fantasy. Trust that any fantasy is an image derived from your experience. It occurred to *you*, didn't it?

Preparing the role of Madame in *The Maids*, you could begin rehearsals with an image of your imperious grandmother, or Diana Ross, or Coco Chanel. Or a southern accent. Or a bad French accent. These are not Genet's images—they are too campy, too

American—but even so, if they come easily to mind, they might help bring you to your own understanding (and successful performance) of the severe irony Genet intended by having ornate baroque language issue from the mouths of dowdy servants and their chic twentieth-century mistress. The style of the production will determine in what ways your campy images are translated into performance. But you needn't begin with what you think are images "appropriate" to the style of the production. You may have no images for severe irony, the baroque phrases may freeze you in your tracks, the ritualized movements the director is wild for may confuse you. Nevertheless, let's say that the idea of Madame's laugh heard offstage makes you think of Jean Harlow in the film *Dinner at Eight* (1933) or, to use a later film as an example, Lesley Anne Warren in *Victor/Victoria* (1982): a cheap *floozy* who, despite being rigged out in diamonds and satin, broadcasts her low class every time she opens her mouth to cackle out a crude laugh. If you've smiled at the thought of this image, it might be worth a try in rehearsal.

If you've never seen *Dinner at Eight*, or if Jean Harlow leaves you cold, the image won't work for you. If it does stir you, for whatever reason, go right ahead and do your bad Jean Harlow imitation. It doesn't mean you are going to perform the role as a stereotype. It means you will *exploit a stereotype in order to explore a character*. You're not necessarily going to stop with the stereotype, you're going to begin there.

The potential to abuse stereotypes is such that it might be advisable to read the last three sentences three more times. With that in mind, please continue.

Yes, exploit clichés

The image of the *floozy*, which we've identified as Jean Harlow in *Dinner at Eight*, is a *cliché*. It comes with its own ready-made ways of walking, speaking, and emphasizing importance. Stanislavsky dismissed these ready-made characters as "stamps," meaning the image made by a rubber stamp, necessarily derivative, imprecise, and growing fainter and cruder with use. The word in Russian is pronounced *shtamp*; say it out loud to get the full sense of Slavic disgust.

Yet, when you work with images in rehearsal—especially fantasy images—these stereotypes/clichés/*shtamps* are to be explored, not squelched. Like the bad sketches that precede a drawing, or the clumsy notes a pianist hits when practicing a sonata, so too the first use of imagery in rehearsal might be crude, or halting, or just plain wrong. But images get you started; that's their usefulness. Images give momentum to rehearsals in ways that working towards a task does not. In painting, you have to start with bright color to get bright color. A careful build of pastel tones does not build to vivid color. It makes gray.

In life, it is dangerous, foolish, and demeaning to categorize people as clichés. When the Russian actor Michael Schepkin told the African-American actor Ira Aldridge that Aldridge's Othello would be more "realistic" if he behaved like a crude savage, the cultivated Schepkin was himself behaving crudely. Aldridge knew from his own experience how stereotypes transform others into objects, rather than individuals. Treated as objects, people can be manipulated without scruples or compassion.

The reason that clichés are a bad habit in life—they make it easy to manipulate the image of someone else—is precisely the reason they are useful for actors using imagery in rehearsals. As a performer you *want* to manipulate images—your own as well as those of others. Aldridge sometimes followed his performances of Othello or King Lear with renditions of minstrel songs like "Jump Jim Crow." He sang these jolly banjo tunes sadly, however, and in a ridiculous dialect—a Brechtian opposition to the five acts of Shakespeare he had just performed. Aldridge would then turn to his audience and speak directly to them about the need for the abolition of slavery and respect for the African race. His performance of clichés was meant to undo clichés. In pursuit of that task, Ira Aldridge used clichés for his own purposes.

Should a rehearsal technique include as bad a habit as thinking in clichés? Yes. An actor who manipulates clichés becomes a lot more sensitive to thinking in clichés in life, much more so than someone who assigns clichés unconsciously. Lying, too, is something an actor does. So is the faking of emotions. Neither lying nor faking is much appreciated offstage, but they are work habits for actors onstage. Opera singers learn to make a sound loud enough to sail over a thirty-piece orchestra, appropriate to the vast spaces in which they work. But they do not speak as loudly when they're conversing on the phone. They don't confuse long distance with stage projection, and you shouldn't confuse the stage with life. Remember not to deal with other people in life as clichés, but do deal with the characters you are about to play in that way—at first, anyway.

We have chosen to begin with a cliché of a *movie star* as the image for Madame: Jean Harlow. There was a real woman by the name of Jean Harlow, but she was nothing like our image of her. She was an intelligent and poised young woman, a devout Christian Scientist. Audiences may have been confused about the difference between her personae on the screen and in life—but Jean Harlow wasn't. Likewise, in our own time, the thoroughly professional Goldie Hawn maintains her trademark ditzy image as a character in film and television, but she is certainly not scatterbrained when she's directing or producing the films in which she stars.

If you begin with a "Jean Harlow" or a "Goldie Hawn," what probably excites you is not the reality of their hard work in life (*"Life upon the wicked stage ain't nothing what a girl supposes"* goes Oscar Hammerstein's lyric from *Showboat* [57]), but the resonance of the images these actresses created, images you will take on for your own purposes in the text.* When it comes to working from images, for once, ignorance *is* bliss. It doesn't matter what the reality of Jean Harlow was, or any other image you pick, be it *powerful horse* (some are shy), *mighty motorcycle* (some are not), or *mysterious gypsy* (not all of them). It's precisely your misunderstanding of an image—your heightened romantic response to it—that makes it useful to you as an actor. If your idea is based on a cliché, fine, just as long as it's *your* cliché. *Your* cliché is significant to *you* because it has some connection with your life. A Chinese philosopher was walking along the riverbank with a friend. Oh, he said, looking down into the water, the fish are enjoying themselves today. You

---

*When Genet's *The Maids* was first performed in Mongolia, the performers of course had no idea who Jean Harlow was (nor Goldie Hawn, for that matter). When it was suggested that Madame was someone who pretended to be something she was not, the actress playing the role came up with her own high-pitched petulance. "The kind of girl who thinks she's a Chinese princess," she said, and chirped like a twittering bird. As rehearsals developed, so did the image, and Madame became a Mongolian girl who wanted to pass, as best she could, for Russian—with a blonde wig.

are not a fish, said his friend, how do you know what a fish can feel? You are not I, said the philosopher, how do you know what I can feel?*

True to life or not, even though you will not necessarily perform the role of Madame as a Jean Harlow-in-*Dinner at Eight* imitation, you might begin your rehearsal idea of Madame in just that way. If you haven't seen *Dinner at Eight*, do. It's funny, and you'll be able to follow what is discussed here more closely. Much more serious images could be used, of course. Madame might remind you of an overly sober woman who in private life is a drunk. Her tight-lipped severity might dissolve into a binge of emotions or a screwed-down bitterness. Still, it's a lot more playful as research, in every sense of the word, to watch *Dinner at Eight* than to study secret lushes.

> *A burst of nervous laughter backstage.* MADAME, *in a fur coat, enters laughing with* SOLANGE *behind her.*

The burst of nervous laughter backstage might begin as a high-pitched cackle associated with the *floozy* image. The fur coat, to your way of thinking, will be a white fox, something frivolous, expensive, and gauche. As Madame enters, she mocks the flowers that her maids have strewn about her bedroom:

> MADAME There's no end to it! Such horrible gladioli, such a sickly pink, and mimosa!

Here's another image for you: pointing to the stuffed vases, Madame's affected hand gestures might be like *twittering birds*. But let's cage the birds for now. In your *floozy* image, your hands can rattle with bracelets.

> MADAME They probably hunt through the market before dawn to get them cheaper. (SOLANGE *helps her off with her coat*)

Madame can drop her expensive coat on the floor. Unseen by Madame, the maid Solange can rescue it. When Bette Davis was rehearsing the film *All About Eve*, the director Joseph L. Mankiewicz—who liked to work from images with his actors—told his star that the role she was playing ". . . was the kind of dame who treats her mink coat like a poncho" (58). If you remember this story, then Bette Davis-in-*All About Eve* will be added to your images for Madame. Yes, images can change rapidly in rehearsal, from Jean Harlow to twittering birds to Bette Davis. If you were working with the image of *overly sober Madame*, she might enter more quietly, tight-lipped with disapproval at the overly gaudy flowers, and her laugh would be grim and tight. For now, though, let's stay with unadulterated *floozy*.

> SOLANGE Madame wasn't too cold?
> MADAME Yes, Solange, I was very cold.

---

*If he wasn't a philosopher he would have said: You are not me.

16

As *floozy*, Madame's voice will be childish and petulant as she describes her visit to Monsieur in jail:

> MADAME I've been trailing through corridors all night long. I've been seeing frozen men and stony faces, but I did manage to catch a glimpse of Monsieur. From a distance. I waved to him.

She might imitate her wave to Monsieur with her fingers folded to the palm: a *bye-bye* gesture, a little girl's gesture.

> MADAME I've only just left the wife of a magistrate. Claire!

If your image of Madame was an *imperious mature woman* (your dowager grandmother?), this line would imply that tea with a judge's wife is commonplace within Madame's social world. The image of *floozy*, however, assigns a different meaning to the same words. Harlow's character in *Dinner at Eight* convinces her thug of a boyfriend to accept an invitation to the dinner of the title in order to meet just such high-society types as a judge's wife. Such a meeting would be a social climber's gleaming trophy.

As you apply your images, the call for Claire would likewise change. From the pursed lips of an *imperious Madame*, the call might be coolly melodious. As *floozy*, Madame's call for Claire will be a nasal whine that stretches the sound into two grating syllables: *Clay-yuh!*

> SOLANGE She's preparing Madame's tea.
> MADAME I wish she'd hurry. I'm ashamed to ask for tea when Monsieur is all alone, without a thing, without food, without cigarettes.

The words "without cigarettes" will help you to establish the image of *floozy Madame*. Imagine the horror for such a Madame—not being able take a drag on a coffin nail! You might even add a loud "*The woist!*" in rehearsal.

Translate the text into the language of the image

You could have picked many other images for Madame: *icy matron, chic fashion-plate, Margaret Thatcher, Evita Perón*. Don't question why you picked this one or that one; it occurred to you, so use it. Still, it's not enough to pick one image, or even several ones. The job of an actor working this way is to *respond to the images of the text or situation with personal metaphors* (which we just did with Harlow)—and then *apply those images by reassigning a value to the rest of the specific words in the play* (which we just did with the cigarettes).

The process of responding with an image is incomplete until the rest of the play is **translated** into the language of the response. Most approaches to acting stress specificity; this approach is no different. Without such specificity, the image will be false and appliquéd—sewn or glued onto the surface.

BUILDING IMAGES

To generalize is to be an idiot. To particularize is the Alone Distinction of Merit. So wrote William Blake in the margin of Joshua Reynolds' *Discourses on Art.* Like the French archaeologists discovering Cleopatra's name on the Rosetta Stone, you want to identify the points of contact between your image and the play's text, and expand from what you know to what you don't know.

It is especially important to translate the other characters and the environment into the language of your image. If Madame is your *imperious grandmother*, the unseen Monsieur is a *gentleman*. If Madame is a *floozy*, the unseen Monsieur is her *thug of a sugar daddy*. If Madame is *Jean Harlow* in *Dinner at Eight*, then Solange can be Jean Harlow's sour-faced maid in the same film. This is not necessarily the image that the actress rehearsing Solange will play, nor should you as *Jean Harlow Madame* expect the other actress to knowingly fulfil your fantasy. Each of the actors will have their own private set of images, evocative to them.

Every actor in the scene will have different images

According to the story of the play, Solange is stalling Madame while the younger maid, Claire, is in the kitchen poisoning Madame's tea. For the actress playing Solange, the image she has of herself might be nothing like a lady's maid, but, rather, a *farm woman* allowing a chicken to run around the yard before Solange seizes it and wrings its neck. If Solange is a *farm woman* preparing to kill a chicken, Madame is that chicken and her talk is just squawk. Solange might hear Madame's cry for Claire as if it were the squeal of a pig, soon to be hung as ham. Solange will maintain a butcher's professionally cool demeanor so as not to alarm the animal about to be slaughtered.

Since the actors have different images of the scene, each will see the other in relationship to that image. The quiet, methodical gestures of Solange's *farm woman* will be interpreted by *Jean Harlow Madame* as those of a crimped *spying maid*. (This parallel could work: Jean Harlow's sour-faced maid blackmails Harlow in *Dinner at Eight*; Madame's maids in Genet's play are likewise blackmailing her. Although Madame doesn't know it, Claire and Solange have sent anonymous letters to incriminate Monsieur. That's why he's in jail.)

> SOLANGE But Monsieur won't stay there long. They'll see right away that he's not guilty.
>
> MADAME Guilty or not, I shall never desert him, never. You see, Solange, it's at times like this that you realize how much you love someone. I don't think he's guilty either, but if he were, I'd become his accomplice. I'd follow him to Devil's Island, to Siberia.

If the Grade-B movie dialogue ("Guilty or not, I shall never desert him, never.") reminds you of the preening self-importance of a soap opera diva or Mrs. Siddons's "huzzing," you could change your image for Madame here. Solange might retain her image, however, calming the unsuspecting Madame before she gets too agitated to drink her poison.

MASKS

SOLANGE There's no need to get panicky. I've seen worse cases acquitted. There was a trial in Bordeaux—

MADAME Do you go to trials? You?

SOLANGE I read *True Detective*. I know these things. It was about a man.

Solange has another image here, a *crime fan* so enthused she can't conceal her expertise. To a more astute Madame, this could be a giveaway that Solange is a criminal, but *floozy Madame* or *huzzing Madame* is too besotted by her own drama to notice Solange's slip.

MADAME You can't compare Monsieur's case. He's been accused of the most idiotic thefts. I know he'll get out of it. All I mean is that, as a result of this preposterous affair, I've come to realize how deeply attached I am to him. Of course, none of this is serious, but if it were, Solange, it would be a joy for me to bear his cross. I'd follow him from place to place, from prison to prison, on foot if need be, as far as the penal colony.

If you kept up the image of the *floozy*, Madame's martyrdom is laughable, like Jean Harlow imitating Sarah Bernhardt. In Genet's play, Madame herself is playing an image here, the *tragic queen*. Towering in her high heels, it's ironic for Madame to claim she'd walk barefoot to Siberia. Notice that by casting herself as the *tragic queen*, Madame is recasting Solange as her *confidante*. At the same time, translated into Solange's language of imagery, Madame's flights of fancy are the scampers of a *nervous pig* in need of curt discipline.

Vocal masks

SOLANGE They wouldn't let you. Only bandits' wives, or their sisters, or their mothers, are allowed to follow them.

MADAME A condemned man is no longer a bandit. And then I'd force my way in, past the guards. (*suddenly coquettish*) And, Solange, I'd be utterly fearless. I'd use my weapons. What do you take me for?

SOLANGE Madame mustn't get such ideas into her head. You must rest.

MADAME I'm not tired. You treat me like an invalid. You're always trying to coddle me and pamper me as if I were dying. Thank God, I've got my wits about me. I'm ready for the fight. (*she looks at* SOLANGE *and, feeling that she has hurt her, adds, with a smile*) Come, come, don't make such a face. (*with sudden violence*) All right, it's true! There are times when you're so sweet that I simply can't stand it.

The words "I simply can't stand it" might remind you of a *sound*: the harsh voice of another cliché of a floozy. There is a very similar line in the film *Singin' in the Rain* (1952), where a screechy silent film star is taking a voice lesson and practicing to say "*I can't stand him*" with hilariously shrill flat "A's" on *can't* and *stand*. If you say Madame's lines

19

in this way, your mouth will stretch back, and the position of your mouth, combined with the shrill pitch of your voice, will make for you a **vocal mask**.

A vocal mask is just that: a way of masking your voice. Vocal masks are created when you change your pitch, or tone, or when you place your voice differently in your throat or mouth; by stretching your lips back in a smile, for example, or lowering your chin. Olivier used vocal masks when he lowered the pitch of his voice almost a full octave for Othello and when he thinned the timbre of his sound playing Richard III. A vocal mask is different from an *accent*. Geography and class determine an accent; it can be studied with precision. Vocal masks can include accents, of course, but they don't need to be *authentic* accents, any more than a carved mask needs to be a realistic face.

If authenticity interests you, you can study technical ways to reproduce accents with some excellent Henry-Higgins-in-reverse books that instruct the reader to say *ryne*, not *rain*. In any case, if you know about accents, those associations will help enormously to carve vocal masks. Imagine a southern accent for Skinny, the henchman in Brecht's *In the Jungle of Cities*, and you have a certain approach to the character. If you know enough to specify the southern accent you'll begin to specify the role. Imagine that Skinny speaks like a native of Tupelo, Mississippi (birthplace of Elvis Presley) in a hard-nosed twangy accent. That's very different from the genteel lilt of someone from Richmond, Virginia (whence comes Robert E. Lee). Employ twangy Tupelo and you have Skinny as a *used car salesman*: insistent, humorous, and pointed in his sales pitch. Utilize lilting Virginia and you have a *gentleman salesman* Skinny, perhaps with an apologetic lifted pitch at the end of sentences, very beguiling with the customers, *very* sorry that Garga isn't taking his good suggestions.

Using a fantasy image frees you to create your own vocal masks, unrestricted by time and place. Your border-crossing Count Dracula or your inconsistent Queen's English (which will drive your speech teacher wild) are appropriate to rehearse with if they induce you to feel the sense of exotic mystery or upper-class arrogance you intend them to create—remember Bernhardt looking at the palms of her own hands?

Certain lines may suggest ready-made line readings: *"I'd use my weapons"* might make you think of the thrust-out chest of the actress Ann-Margret, known in the 1960s as "the kitten-with-a-whip," a nickname that itself might provoke an image and a sub-vocalized sound like a cat's *meow*. *"What do you take me for?"* might evoke the shrill silent film star in *Singin' in the Rain* who memorably says: *"What d'ya think I am? Dumb or something?"*

Even though the text of *The Maids* is a translation—and a British one at that, with class associations like "tay" for "tea"—the words can still give you your own ideas about which vocal masks to try on in rehearsal. The emphases of the vocal mask assign value to the words, such as Madame's "without cigarettes" or "I simply can't stand it." In the lines of Madame's entrance—"There's no end to it! Such horrible gladioli, such a sickly pink, and mimosa!"—the sharp *i*'s of *mimosa* and *sickly*, and the over-pronunciation of *gladioli* will emphasize Madame's daintiness.

Once you establish the emphases given by the vocal mask, you should rehearse with the mask long enough for it to become comfortable. As rehearsals progress, you might make a choice to alter the vocal mask. This process is often described as *dropping the ac-*

cent, but the word "dropping" is misleading. The emphases of the mask are not abandoned; rather, some aspects are kept, some are not. For example, the lilting flirtatiousness of a southern accent might be retained along with its emphasis in certain words and meanings—even though the twang and the diphthongs would be eliminated. Madame's daintiness would stay; the sharp *i*'s would go.

Work from the outside in

Physical aspects of the rehearsal or performance may trigger inner images.

> MADAME It crushes me, stifles me! And those flowers which are there for the very opposite of a celebration!
>
> SOLANGE If Madame means that we lack discretion . . .
>
> MADAME But I didn't mean anything of the kind, honey. It's just that I'm so upset. You see what a state I'm in.
>
> SOLANGE Would Madame like to see the day's accounts?
>
> MADAME You certainly picked the right time. You must be mad. Do you think I could look at the figures now? Show them to me tomorrow.
>
> SOLANGE (*putting away the fur*) The lining's torn. I'll take it to the furrier tomorrow.

In the vocabulary of Solange's *Madame-as-chicken* image, the animal about to be plucked seems ill at ease; it senses something's about to happen. As she's putting away the fur, Solange can be musing philosophically on the transient nature of life, smiling to herself at the thought that tomorrow Madame will be dead. The *feel* of that fur will evoke certain images for the actress: the luxury and cushion of Madame's life—or the fate of the animal about to be harvested for its skin. These feelings, which will be repeated in rehearsal and performance, can be a signpost (like Cleopatra's name on the Rosetta Stone) to direct your thinking.

Touch can be a very effective trigger for an actor: the heft of expensive crystal, the scratch of coarse wool. Especially evocative images come from the feel of wearing certain clothes. Helene Weigel wore her drab *Mother Courage* dress and boots from the first day of rehearsal. Genet's text for *The Maids* gives Madame an excuse to wear flamboyant costumes, which will reinforce your flamboyant internal images. If your Madame enters tightly corseted, hair piled high on her head, breasts pushed up, and hips pitched vertically due to her high-heel shoes, it's a fair guess that—woman or man—you will *feel* differently. You may not wear six-inch spikes in performance—or even in too many rehearsals—but towering precariously over the other actors will change your relationship to them.

The most obvious of outer masks to trigger an inner image is, of course, the *sight of yourself*. Dressed soberly as Solange, your hair pulled back, feet cased in flat and ugly shoes, and your collar buttoned up, you will feel like a drab lady's maid. If you look at yourself in the mirror you will *see* a drab lady's maid. There are some performers who are thrown off balance when they look in the mirror. At the sight of their own reflection, they become too critical of the differences between Jean Harlow and themselves. The vitality of their image is kept when the image is kept internal. For them, the *feel* of the clothing is more than enough to build a character.

But if staring at yourself leads to inner reflection and onstage action, don't be shy: go right ahead and stare. There are very good precedents. In the Japanese theater, actors have a special room where they go before performances just to gaze at themselves in the mirror. Stanislavsky wrote admiringly about how Salvini would spend three hours before he went on as Othello: putting on his make-up and turban in front of the mirror, then coming out to wander the stage or the wings, more and more in the image of the character by the alternation of physical and internal preparation. By the way, Eleonora Duse died in Pittsburgh because she came to the theater to prepare three-and-a-half hours before an eight o'clock performance. She had walked from her hotel to the stage door (which was locked) in a rainstorm. Once she got inside the theater, no one was there to turn on the heat and Duse caught pneumonia. (Sometimes, it's better you prepare your image at home.)

As you sit and stare at yourself in the mirror, you wait to be given an internal clue from the external, like the sculptor who looks at the block of marble in order to see the sculpture inside it. Michelangelo worked like this in stone. It's also how Eskimo carvers work in ivory. Such preparation is not free-association; rather, you are looking for a *direction* from the material. For the Eskimo it's a walrus tusk, for the performer it's your face, or your body. Looking in the mirror develops your intuitive sensitivity to the language of your images.

Stringing the masks

SOLANGE (*putting away the fur*) The lining's torn. I'll take it to the furrier tomorrow.

MADAME If you like. Though it's hardly worthwhile. I'm giving up my wardrobe. Besides, I'm an old woman.

SOLANGE There go those gloomy ideas again.

MADAME I'm thinking of going into mourning. Don't be surprised if I do. How can I lead a worldly life when Monsieur is in prison? If you find the house too sad . . .

SOLANGE We'll never desert Madame.

MADAME I know you won't, Solange. You've not been too unhappy with me, have you?

SOLANGE Oh!

MADAME When you needed anything, I saw that you got it. With my old gowns alone you both could have dressed like princesses. Besides . . . (*she goes to the closet and looks at her dresses*) of what use will they be to me? I'm through with finery and all that goes with it.

CLAIRE *enters carrying the tea.*

MASKS

A liberating aspect of working with images is that their sequence does not have to be logical in its progression any more than the scenes of a text have to follow strict chronological order for a playwright to tell the story of a play. You can begin with the afternoon, move to the dawn, and then go to the evening if those are the images that apply. In this way, working with images does resemble a dream; just as time melts, so does form. Jean Harlow can morph into Sarah Bernhardt. Your fantasy General can dissolve into a fantasy Samurai Warrior. Just as roles change from scene to scene, so too do masks. The string of masks you carve in rehearsal will have its own vocabulary. Notice it. In the example from *The Maids*, Madame is composed of *diva* images: Jean Harlow, Ann-Margret, Sarah Bernhardt, Lesley Anne Warren. Knowing that this is your language—leading ladies—you may add others. Josephine Baker? Mei Lanfang? Dustin Hoffman as *Tootsie*?

Another string might be composed of *imitations*: Jean Harlow pretending to be Sarah Bernhardt. A Mongolian woman pretending to be Russian. Ira Aldridge in white-face as Macbeth. Laurence Olivier in black-face as Othello. Dustin Hoffman in Tootsie's red dress. The juxtaposition of masks will be intuitive, not logical or planned. As in episodic structure, image follows image without cause and effect. It isn't necessary to connect the images you are working with to one larger "guiding" image. However, it is good technique to play an image fully before moving to the next one, and to demonstrate changes in imagery so that the audience can sense, if not actually identify, the difference.

Too often in a performance an interesting image will be created in the first scene without any follow-through: the image repeats but doesn't *develop* during the course of the play. Even if you choose to play more than one image, you should develop each one somewhat before you drop it for the next one. As the Pupil of Ionesco's *Lesson* ends her tutorial, she should arrive at an image transformed from the one with which she started. The character of the unhappily pregnant Hedda Gabler who kills herself in the fourth act would be built out of images different from the images that built the character of the assured newlywed Hedda in the first act.

There is a dimension of time to images, just as there is a dimension of time to all aspects of theater. If you are working from a *scent*, for example (*sour towels* for Solange, *expensive perfume* for Madame), at what stage of the scent are you? How does the scent develop as the play progresses? A scent hits your nose, blooms, fades off, lingers in the air, and disappears—except as a memory.

Even a cliché should have some development. Are you *Bugs Bunny* at home eating a carrot? Fleeing the hunter? Outwitting the hunter? Hopping off into the distance? Or: *Jean Harlow* in the bath? On the phone? At that eight o'clock soiree? Is your *Tina Turner* playing it rough? Or taking it nice and easy? As the play progresses, images should—and will—develop and change just as Strindberg described: *the characters split, double, multiply, evaporate, condense, disperse, assemble.*

Using an image in rehearsal, even if you discard or advance past it, will add to the depth of your characterization in performance, just as preparing sketches adds depth to a finished artwork. You may find that upon reflection certain images don't really apply to a particular role or text, or are so potent to you that they can be used in other roles and in other plays. Olivier claimed to store details of observed behavior and ideas for as long as eighteen years (59). They became part of his *personal history*, the subject of the next chapter. Those partisans of the Method and Olivier had more in common than either would admit.

Let's Review Terms

images	personal metaphors that answer the question *What is this like?*
fantasy images	imaginary images that excite you to perform
personal history	images remembered from your past
translating images	converting an actor's images to the images of the text
vocal mask	a characteristic way of speaking
to string masks	to assemble a character from a collection of images

The Chart

Let's begin to fill out the chart for the techniques of *Building Images*.

- **Basic unit.** The basic unit is the *image*, the actor's personal metaphor for elements of the text including characters and events, as well as details like costume, sound, and situations.
- **Key question.** The image should answer the actor's question *What is this like?* Or: *What does this make me think of?*
- **The intended reaction of the audience.** The audience is meant to become *passionate* as they respond to a performer's image with images of their own.
- **The relative theory.** The Swiss psychologist *Carl Jung* theorized that character is made of shifting images, like a string of masks, which he called *personae*.

Notebook: Building Images

A burst of nervous laughter backstage.
MADAME, *in a fur coat, enters laughing with*
SOLANGE *behind her.*

MADAME There's no end to it! Such horrible gladi-oli, such a sickly pink, and mimosa! They probably hunt through the market before dawn to get them cheaper. (SOLANGE *helps her off with her coat*)

SOLANGE Madame wasn't too cold?

MADAME Yes, Solange, I was very cold. I've been trailing through corridors all night long. I've been seeing frozen men and stony faces, but I did manage to catch a glimpse of Monsieur. From a distance. I waved to him. I've only just left the wife of a magistrate. <u>Claire!</u>

SOLANGE She's preparing Madame's tea.

MADAME I wish she'd hurry. I'm ashamed to ask for tea when Monsieur is all alone, without a thing, without food, <u>without cigarettes.</u>

SOLANGE But Monsieur won't stay there long. They'll see right away that he's not guilty.

MADAME Guilty or not I shall never desert him, never. You know, Solange, it's at times like this that you realize how much you love someone. I don't think he's guilty either, but if he were, I'd become his accomplice. I'd follow him to Devil's Island, to Siberia.

SOLANGE There's no need to get panicky. I've seen worse cases acquitted. There was a trial in Bordeaux—

MADAME Do you go to trials? You?

SOLANGE I read *True Detective*. I know these things. It was about a man who—

(Notes for both roles, Madame and Solange)

Madame is Jean Harlow in *Dinner at Eight*.

A squeaky laugh. A cheap floozy rigged out in diamonds and satin, but still low class when she opens her mouth.

Solange is the sour-faced blackmailing maid from *Dinner at Eight*

(Solange's image: Solange is a farm woman allowing a chicken to run around the yard before she seizes it and wrings its neck)

(To Solange's image, Madame's cry <u>Claire!</u> is like the squeal of a pig)

<u>without cigarettes</u>: The woist!

Harlow miscast in a tragic role, but gamely trying. Playing the Tragic Queen—Sarah Bernhardt? Solange turned into the confidante.

(Solange's image: the gushing fan, but Madame is too self-involved to notice the slip)

BUILDING IMAGES

MADAME You can't compare Monsieur's case. He's been accused of the most idiotic thefts. I know he'll get out of it. All I mean is that, as a result of this preposterous affair, I've come to realize how deeply attached I am to him. Of course, none of this is serious, but if it were, Solange, it would be a joy for me to bear his cross. I'd follow him from place to place, from prison to prison, on foot if need be, as far as the penal colony.

Appreciating her own performance as serious actress. Childishly surprised at her serious side: God, who knew I was so deep!

SOLANGE They wouldn't let you. Only bandits' wives, or their sisters, or their mothers, are allowed to follow them.

Madame is a twelve-year-old brat

MADAME A condemned man is no longer a bandit. And then I'd force my way in, past the guards. *(suddenly coquettish)* And, Solange, I'd be utterly fearless. <u>I'd use my weapons.</u> What do you take me for?

Solange as spoil-sport

SOLANGE Madame musn't get such ideas into her head. You must rest.

Madame wrinkling her face up like a thwarted child. (Solange's image: an expert) <u>I'd use my weapons</u>: Ann-Margret.

MADAME I'm not tired. You treat me like an invalid. You're always trying to coddle me and pamper me as if I were dying. Thank God, I've got my wits about me. I'm ready for the fight. *(She looks at* SOLANGE *and, feeling that she has hurt her, adds, with a smile)* Come, come, don't make such a face. *(with sudden violence)* All right, it's true! There are times when you're so sweet that <u>I simply can't stand it</u>. It crushes me, stifles me! And those flowers which are there for the very opposite of a celebration!

Solange as older sister.

Madame as sulky child on a rainy day, like a little girl talking with her dolls.

SOLANGE If Madame means that we lack discretion . . .

MADAME But I didn't mean anything of the kind, honey. It's just that I'm so upset. You see what a state I'm in.

<u>I can't stand it</u>: like the same line from *Singin' in the Rain*.

SOLANGE Would Madame like to see the day's accounts?

(Solange's image: the animal to be slaughtered seems to sense something's up)

Like a little girl trying on hats.

MADAME You certainly picked the right time. <u>You must be mad.</u> Do you think I could look at the figures now? Show them to me tomorrow.

<u>You must be mad</u>: A little girl playing with a "Lady's" hat. *(She would usually say, "Are you nuts?")*

26

SOLANGE (*putting away the fur*) The lining's torn. I'll take it to the furrier tomorrow.

MADAME If you like. Though it's hardly worthwhile. I'm giving up my wardrobe. Besides, I'm an old woman.

SOLANGE There go those gloomy ideas again.

MADAME I'm thinking of going into mourning. Don't be surprised if I do. How can I lead a worldly life, when Monsieur is in prison? If you find the house too sad . . .

SOLANGE We'll never desert Madame.

MADAME I know you won't, Solange. You've not been too unhappy with me, have you?

SOLANGE Oh!

MADAME When you needed anything, I saw that you got it. With my old gowns alone you both could have dressed like princesses. Besides . . . (*She goes to the closet and looks at her dresses*) Of what use will they be to me? I'm through with finery and all that goes with it.

Claire enters carrying the tea.

(putting away the fur) *(Solange's image: Musing philosophically on the transient nature of life, smiling to herself at the thought that tomorrow Madame will be dead)*

I'm thinking of going into mourning:
Like little girl playing with a black veil, a caprice. Waving her hands in excitement as if drying her nail polish. Like a new decorating scheme.

When you needed anything:
Little girl playing with a hat from a charity ball.

I'm through with finery: Like a girl playing with a nun's whimple.

(Claire's image: the unsmiling executioner intent on her task)

27

CHAPTER 2

The Language of Images

Polus and the Urn

Polus was an actor who lived in ancient Greece around the fifth century BCE, the first performer in history to be recorded as having had an acting technique. You would think he'd be better known for it. What did Polus do? He brought a funeral urn that contained his own dead son's ashes onstage with him, so that when he had to weep, he'd have something to cry about.

We think we know what lines Polus was reciting at the time: Electra mourning her brother Orestes, in iambic verse written by Sophocles. Electra's Ancient Grecian formula seems a little remote to you, you say? The verse just doesn't grab you? That's the point. It didn't grab Polus that much either, so he substituted something that did: the *emotional memory* of his dead son.

In America, beginning in the 1930s, acting teachers led by Lee Strasberg seized on substitution and emotional memory and made these techniques the foundation of honest acting, which they called the Method. Though most Method actors claim adherence to Stanislavsky (as channeled through Strasberg), the notion of identifying the sole source of onstage behavior as personal imagery provoked Stanislavsky to an angry rebuke when the same thing happened in Russia twenty years before Strasberg. As early as 1913, Stanislavsky sharply criticized one of his disciples, Vahktangov, for directing actors from a base of emotional memory into "emotional hysteria, acting in a trance, performing for themselves, not the audience" (60).

Stanislavsky's rejection of emotional memory as hysteria is similar in tone and vocabulary to Sigmund Freud's rejection of his followers' attempts to unleash hysteria under hypnosis. Both Stanislavsky and Freud were trying to create a rational system for analysis and develop a set of repeatable procedures for change. Both men disliked "inspiration" as an explanation, although both respected inspiration as a phenomenon and recognized it in themselves. Both felt that succumbing to an image or the energy released by an emotional block was a confusing diversion from the scientific, or, in Stanislavsky's case, craftsman's approach.

Strasberg was aware of Stanislavsky's displeasure. As was discussed in Chapter 3, when Stella Adler brought back criticism to Strasberg from Stanislavsky himself, Strasberg stuck to his guns—and to his Method. Over time, other acting teachers who had derived their own techniques from Stanislavsky made a point to distance themselves from Strasberg's approach and from the label of "Method" acting, similar to the way Piscator distanced himself from the term *epic theater* in order to avoid an association with Brecht.

Among Method actors, the emphases on emotional memory and personal history are variously called advancements, improvements, and adjustments of Stanislavsky's ideas. The strong tone of a good defense runs through their intolerance: *never use imitation, never begin with a cliché, never prepare in a mirror.* Due to the professional success of Method actors in America—among them Julie Harris, Paul Newman, Geraldine Page, Eli Wallach, Dustin Hoffman, Al Pacino, even Marilyn Monroe—Strasberg became famous and Method partisans spoke with the faith of convinced zealots, insisting on the uniqueness and naturalness of their school. Stella Adler students—Robert De Niro and Marlon Brando among them—who include fantasies among their personal images, are more modest about their training, which perhaps reflects that Adler taught actors to bring themselves to the role, not the role to themselves.

The clashes between the Method and other schools are the source of many good anecdotes. The best is between Laurence Olivier and Dustin Hoffman. In the one film they made together, *Marathon Man* (1976), Olivier played a sadistic dentist who was a former Nazi, and Hoffman played his hapless victim. One day Hoffman showed up on the set red-eyed and haggard. To prepare for the scene they were shooting, Hoffman had stayed sleepless and run around the block until he was as exhausted as the character he was playing. Noticing this, Olivier said, "Why don't you try acting, dear boy. It's far easier" (59). Yet when Olivier's will was read, it revealed that Olivier had bequeathed the false teeth he'd worn as Shylock to Dustin Hoffman. Having nothing to defend but excellence, Olivier could afford to be generous.

Let's examine the Method, then, denying its uniqueness (Polus did it first, two millennia earlier) but appreciating its effectiveness. In our vocabulary, the Method is a system of acting choices based on the imagery of *personal history*.

American Enthusiasm for Personal Images

Method actors claim a performer's use of personal history is so natural that all actors have done it at all times, knowingly or not. This is no more true (or false) than Stanislavsky's belief that all good actors already used his system of tasks, or Brecht's claim that Stanislavsky was staging epic theater. The desire to have one theory explain all others is one more example that, even though human behavior seems to stay the same through the ages, *interpretations* of human behavior depend on what observers have the chance to see, and when and where they see it.

American enthusiasm for images of personal experience can perhaps be understood better by considering what was happening in America during the years after the Second World War. This was the period when the Group Theatre led by Strasberg fell apart and was replaced by the Actors Studio in 1947 as a place for like-minded theater professionals to experiment with their craft.

Conformity and rebellion

After the Second World War ended in 1945, the United States entered a period of growth and material progress. The country was buoyed by military success, protected by superior weapons and a short-lived monopoly of the atomic bomb. The mechanical inventions of the earlier half of the century—electric power, the automobile, cinema, radio, phonograph records, and television—spread throughout the country. Foreign demand for these and other American products gave the United States political and economic influence throughout the world.

At the same time, America's expansion was shadowed by the growth of a competing power, the Soviet Union. Russia's Communist government proclaimed its own ambitions to influence the world, on behalf of the working class and poverty-stricken people left behind by capitalism's division of society into haves and have-nots. In 1949 Russia exploded its own atomic bomb, shattering America's monopoly and escalating the potential for a conflict. Arguments between the super-powers never grew beyond skirmishes and face-offs, but the threat of collision, and the possibility of nuclear destruction, created a bunker mentality in both countries.

Method acting derived from a Russian master, and its earliest American followers, like other artists and intellectuals around the world, tended to flirt with Communism in the 1930s. Whether they were naïve or delusional is a matter for debate, but their sympathy for the Soviet Union made them vulnerable in the era of Cold War politics. As early as 1939, they had seen the Federal Theater Project stripped of its funding by the innuendo of the House Un-American Activities Committee. This is one reason, perhaps, why Strasberg's followers emphasized the American—rather than the Russian—character of their technique. In Cold War America, those suspected of Communist sympathies were denied work. Those convicted of Communist party membership were jailed. The moguls of the entertainment business—enthusiastic capitalists all—understood their responsibilities as image makers and patriotically policed themselves against Communist sympathizers with industry blacklists.

The rumors of Communist oppression and the intention to spread that oppression were used to justify an uncomplaining compliance with social rules and roles, not only in the entertainment industry but in other aspects of American life as well. The postwar era remembered nostalgically for its stability was also a time of suffocating conformity. There were obvious imperfections in the American system, but attempts at reshaping society were interpreted as foreign-inspired attacks.

Most successful American plays, movies, songs, and paintings of the period catered to the majority of the audience happy to accentuate the positive aspects of growth and ignore what was ugly, ignorant, or unpleasant. In popular film, characters who broke the social rules or defied social roles came to a bad end, usually with just enough time to repent. Women who broke marriage vows or taboos of virginity were particularly doomed by plot devices to serve as examples for other women watching in the audience. The forms of mass culture that did present images of an alternative America at this time—biker movies, science-fiction films, and *film noir*—identified rebels, outsiders, and lawbreakers as losers doomed to fail or die. Sweet, positive, and altruistic characters succeeded in life because they deserved to.

In America, Method acting's reliance on the uniquely personal images of experience was attractive to those with a taste for originality. Creation of personal images had a further attraction in that the source of creativity was within the individual. This was a way for actors to make their art rebel against a conformist society and popular sentimental art.

Abstract Expressionist painters

There was a rebellion in the other arts, too, that fulfilled the American search for individuality among the rank and file. Among painters, the results were dramatic and startling. After four decades of debate in America about what to depict—Connecticut meadows or gritty slums, society matrons or prostitutes—avant-garde American artists after the Second World War chose to depict nothing at all.

"If you want to see a face, go look at one," said Jackson Pollock, the most willfully daring of them all (61). Pollock hurled, threw, dripped, and dribbled paint against his canvasses. The compositions formed were abstract. They didn't look like anything but themselves, and Pollock didn't intend them to. Other painters devised their own techniques. Franz Kline swept broad paint strokes of meaningless calligraphy across large white canvasses. Mark Rothko applied thin washes of paint to create abstract blocks of color. Although ridiculed by a public that preferred the clichés of illustrations, these painters were championed by perceptive critics and named the *Abstract Expressionists*. The traditional techniques of representational painting were unnecessary to their work. The paintings themselves were the subjects, not representations of something else. Although these artists had studied drawing and, in some cases, mastered the art of representation, they chose to create new ways to paint. "Technique is the result of saying something," Pollock said, "not vice versa" (61).

The rise of the avant-garde American jazz music called *be-bop* underscored Pollock's drive to free his art from old techniques. The word *be-bop* is a combination of nonsense syllables that refers to the bounce (*be bop!*) given to a melody, sometimes bent beyond recognition. Relatively unconcerned with the composer's intentions, *bop* musicians brought a personal response to their musical interpretations. During onstage improvisations, *bop* artists such as the trumpeter Dizzy Gillespie, or the pianist Thelonious Monk, or the alto saxophonist Charlie "Bird" Parker conversed among themselves with their instruments, developing a private musical language that was unconcerned with mass popularity or audience approval. Improvisation among jazz musicians dates back to the earliest days of jazz, but after the Second World War *bop* made improvisation central to performance, not ornamental or peripheral. These musicians' experimentation took them beyond the traditional Western scales to exotic chromatic harmonies.

But even while abstaining from traditional techniques, avant-garde painters and *bop* musicians did not diminish rigorous standards. The Abstract Expressionists often mastered traditional painting techniques before rejecting them in favor of brilliant and original methods. The *bop* musicians were accomplished and sophisticated craftsmen, and had scorn for enthusiastic amateurs. By contrast, actors who rebelled against traditional acting techniques often refused to learn their craft. They based the form of their work exclusively on the images of their experiences and ignored the discipline recommended or required by older traditions. They rebelled against elocution lessons, the practice of graceful stage movement, and the study of stage history and literature. Among some performers, personal suffering was considered an adequate enough substitute for the hard work of personal development. A revival of romantic thought ran through it all: an artist's deeply felt emotions were all that one needed to create unique, expressive forms. Everything else would follow—appropriate gestures, interpretation of lines, even diction and volume—if the actor stayed true to the expression of the impulses of passion.

This rebellion in form and process extended to rehearsals and performances that were unbound by social decorum. Actors grunted and scratched themselves. They mumbled their lines, yawned, or paused in the middle of sentences. Scratches and grunts and thoughtful pauses were a part of life and therefore were not to be excluded by anyone seeking to create truth with gestures and sounds on stage or screen. Fantasy, imitation, and clichés were rejected as copies of someone else's life.

The paintings of Abstract Expressionism didn't offer models for a performer the way Grosz's political cartoons informed the gestures of episodic acting, or Repin's nuanced social awareness shaped Stanislavsky's revelation of human relationships. Nevertheless, the *process* of Abstract Expressionism was, and is, a model for the *process* of performers using personal history. Expression begins within the painter—not with observation of the world or a technique for reproduction—just as an actor using personal history begins with the images of his own experience and memories rather than those described by the playwright.

Technology improves communication

An important factor in the rise of an actor's use of personal expression was the development of recording and broadcasting equipment. Slight vocal nuances and even sub-vocalizations that would have gone unheard in a theater could now contribute to a performance in film or on radio. Gestures and facial expressions that would have been unseen at a distance if they were up on a stage, could now, with the help of a close-up or a well-placed camera, become sources of strength in a performance in a film. If only an actor could *express* emotion, the camera and the microphone could do the job of communicating that expression to an audience. The ability of microphones to relay intimate expression affected other performing arts, especially popular music.

Sinatra

Strong personal expression grew not only among post-war jazz musicians, but among American popular singers as well. As great as they were, earlier popular singers like Louis Armstrong or Bing Crosby did not often offer themselves up personally in their interpretations. The next generation of American singers who reached their peak in the 1950s—Billie Holiday, Judy Garland, and Frank Sinatra are examples—sang out of their own experiences and openly identified with their lyrics, even those of standards that had been sung by hundreds of people before them. Improved microphones allowed for a more intimate tone, and singers took advantage of the opportunity to express themselves.

For an example, listen to Sinatra's 1955 album *In the Wee Small Hours*, a suite of songs describing the pain of a man going through a separation from a woman. Bob Hilliard and Dave Mann's title song is as intimate as a dramatic monologue. Sinatra's identification with the material was obvious; it was widely known that he had recently broken up with his second wife, the sultry, glamorous, and alcoholic screen actress Ava Gardner—with whom he had a famously tempestuous relationship. The titles of the songs that make up the suite are revealing:

- "Glad to Be Unhappy"
- "I Get Along Without You Very Well"
- "When Your Lover Has Gone"
- "I'll Never Be the Same"

When Sinatra was a pure-voiced boy, his early recordings of love songs had an intimate quality, but his brave self-exploration on this later album enriched the music and deepened the listener's experience. In 1955, Sinatra was forty years old and his sound was no longer sweet; his instrument was ravaged from the pain of living and all the more expressive for its imperfections. If he had been a singer of the old school and performing onstage without a microphone, Sinatra might have finessed through the rough spots, making up in volume what he had lost in quality. Even if he hadn't, the subtle tarnish and cracks in his sound would have been lost to the distance in a theater. But such subtleties and flaws are just what the microphone collects and the record preserves. On this album, without the need to project or protect himself, Sinatra reveals each self-examining song's emotional truth. The result is an affecting model for the use of personal history in a performance. Frank Sinatra could also apply personalization to other kinds of performing. The year before this album was recorded, he won an Oscar as best supporting actor for his non-singing role in the film *From Here to Eternity* (1953).

Psychological blocks

In conformist 1950s America, creativity was identified with tapping into a personal source, often of pain and anger. In acting, in music, or in painting, the creative process was one of mining the subconscious—not only to express it, but to free it from itself. A person's traumatic experiences were understood to be stored as tension that blocked feeling and free expression in the body and the brain. Often the goal of the psychologist, the artist, or the actor was to hunt down and dig into these *psychological blocks*.

A theory of uncovering psychological blocks was elaborated by another of Freud's renegade disciples, Wilhelm Reich. After much experimentation, Freud had rejected the therapeutic use of uncovering blocks. He believed that uncovered blocks could only be experienced as sensations and, ultimately, provided no more insight than hypnotic states.

Reich and later psychologists hoped to break down psychological blocks in order to release a flood of dammed-up emotions, which would then free patients to express themselves. The techniques developed for therapeutic breakdowns ranged from deep breathing, storytelling, sex, electroshock, hallucinogenic drugs, screaming, and, yes, hypnosis. The theory held that once blocks were removed, the true character of a person revealed itself, displaying the shadow personae (an idea borrowed from Jung) that lay behind the public and social masks, not only of the face, but of the entire body.* Suppressed and festering memories would come to the surface of awareness. Motives that had stayed dark secrets would be recognized and spoken out loud.

Popular entertainment in America was quick to exploit the idea of psychological blocks, suppressed memory, and secret personae. In films and plays, trauma victims recovered from amnesia, psychotics revealed their hidden motives, and ordinary people discovered poetic depth when psychological blocks were identified and removed. From movie thrillers to serious-minded plays, traumatic experiences provided a shorthand for understanding more complex problems.

Psychological playwrights

Even among the most celebrated American plays of the post-war era, traumatic moments stand out as significant plot devices. Post-war American playwrights included flashbacks and the recovery of traumatic experiences to explain behavior and establish character. A son's discovery of his father's infidelity in Arthur Miller's *Death of a Salesman* (1949) explains that son's lifelong failure to compete. A wife's discovery of her beloved husband's homosexuality in Tennessee Williams's *A Streetcar Named Desire* (1947) explains her subsequent nymphomania. The techniques of Method acting fulfilled the requirements to act these plays, and the emotional depth of the performers prompted writers to include passages that revealed character in flashbacks and previously repressed memories. A further incentive for an American actor to use personal images: it got you a job.

At this same time in post-war Germany, Bertolt Brecht was writing rigorously political plays. In post-war England, an entire generation of playwrights trained their eyes to observe and dramatize the decline of the British Empire. In France, a group of playwrights played with elaborated fantasy images to create what has been called the *theatre of the absurd*. In all these countries it was felt that diction, volume, and knowing your lines were still the primary skills demanded of an actor. The exclusive use of images from personal history was declared, often correctly, as self-indulgent, and incorrectly as appropriate for a limited repertory of American plays. Images based on an actors' experience can be successfully applied to embody the texts of playwrights who are not American, of course, yet who specifically use memory, flashbacks, or trauma in their writing. Method acting has much to be criticized for—especially its willful ignorance of stagecraft—but it is not true that it is limited to the American post-war psychological plays.

When relying on fantasy images, an actor's task is to use personal imagery as a

---

*With use, these masks could harden, like a callus, into what Reich called *body armor*.

Rosetta Stone to translate the requirements of a text, in addition to being heard and seen. Translating is still the challenge, and always will be, for actors using imagery.

Translating Personal Images: Rehearsing a Scene from *Yerma*

Let's explore an actor's images from personal history and identify some of the specialized terms used to describe their use as if we were rehearsing the last scene of Federico García Lorca's 1934 play *Yerma*. Lorca was a Spanish playwright and poet from the southern city of Grenada. His lifelong themes were the vast passions that erupt when natural impulses are thwarted. His four greatest plays, all set in his home region of heat-baked Andalusia, are *Blood Wedding*, *Doña Rosita*, *The House of Bernarda Alba*, and *Yerma*. Performing Lorca convincingly is one of the greatest challenges in the world repertory. Acting these texts requires a level of emotional commitment that must be believably fervent, neither melodramatic nor subtle.

Lorca invented the name *Yerma*. In Spanish, it means "barren" and it's related to the word for "wasteland." Yerma is also the title character, a woman who burns to have a child. She describes herself in the last scene of the play—the scene where she kills her husband for refusing her a child:

> YERMA I'm like a dry field where a thousand pairs of oxen plow, and you offer me a little glass of well water. Mine is a sorrow already beyond the flesh.
>
> OLD WOMAN (*strongly*) Then stay that way—if you want to! Like the thistles in a dry field, pinched, barren!
>
> YERMA (*strongly*) Barren, yes, I know it! Barren! You don't have to throw it in my face. Nor come to amuse yourself, as youngsters do, in the suffering of a tiny animal. Ever since I married, I've been avoiding that word, and this is the first time I've heard it, the first time it's been said to my face. The first time I see it's the truth.

Even translated from Spanish, without the sound reinforcing the sense, these are passionate and evocative words. If you yourself have wanted a child and that happiness has been denied you, then perhaps your entry to the role will be easier. But even if you haven't had that life experience, using images from other experiences that you have had can help you portray this character of Yerma—personalizing what being barren means to *you*, not only to the made-up character with the made-up name who speaks so beautifully.

Sense memory

> YERMA I'm like a dry field where a thousand pairs of oxen plow, and you offer me a little glass of well water.

Thirst is a common enough experience. With a little coaxing from an actor, the extraordinary thirst that Yerma compares herself to can unfold from this ordinary feeling.

BUILDING IMAGES

When in your life have you really felt parched? Can you remember the particulars of the occasion? The way the back of your throat felt, the way your tongue lay stiff and broken in your mouth? Can you recall a specific time when you were desperate for a sip of water? In childhood? Before you were seven? Before you could speak?

The specificity of the memory will increase if you investigate the experience in your memory. But if nothing comes to mind—if it has been a long time since you've been so thirsty—perhaps you might do a simple preparation by not drinking very much for several days, or drinking nothing at all for several hours. Then take a walk in the sun. Feel the sweat trickling down your forehead? Taste it. It's salty and it adds to your thirst. Feel the heat of the light on your cheekbones? Feel the dust lining your windpipe? Sit near a fountain, but don't allow yourself to take a drink. Watch the other people drinking. Notice your own feelings as you watch them satisfy their thirst.

You will begin with a cluster of sensations—the heat, the taste of your sweat—in order to build a **sense memory**. Rather than guess what the yellow dirt of Spain looks like without rain, rather than invent what it would be like to be thirsty, you will experience real thirst in order to remember the sensations and so be able to call up the experience later, perhaps when you are onstage. The hot lights of the theater might trigger the memory of the hot day when you went without water and enviously watched the fountain drinkers.

You will not, however, show up for a performance seriously dehydrated. That kind of self-manipulation is amateurish and self-defeating. If you are delirious with thirst under the hot theater lights, you may have a genuinely desperate experience that parallels Yerma's, but you won't have the strength to complete your professional responsibilities like speaking the lines, responding to cues, and positioning your gestures so they can be seen by the audience. It is this aspect of an actor's job that Olivier meant when he playfully suggested to Dustin Hoffman: *Try acting*. A genuinely exhausted actor cannot usually apply the inner image to his performance. With rare exceptions, such a performance remains its own non-translated hieroglyphic.

This may be permissible on camera, because the intelligence of a film performance is in the hands of the editor and director. Some actors' lack of stage awareness can be compensated for on a film set by the adjustment of microphones and a shift in camera angles, rather than an appeal to the performer's craft. The job of providing material to record on film can be met in a variety of ways. In the early days of film, before he made *Orphans of the Storm*, D.W. Griffith ordered pins stuck into babies to make them cry. One of the most promising young Method actresses in the early 1950s gave herself gangrene by sticking pins in her legs as a preparation for class. Baby or adult, it's better—and less painful—to be the type of actor who can *act*, not merely someone whose performance is induced or needs to be salvaged by a director, editor, and technical crew.

To continue with the scene from *Yerma*:

OLD WOMAN You make me feel no pity. None. I'll find another woman for
my boy.

The OLD WOMAN *leaves. A great chorus is heard distantly, sung by the pilgrims.*

THE LANGUAGE OF IMAGES

When used appropriately, sense memory allows an actor to access a feeling and bring it onstage during the performance of the play. For example, the stage direction *a great chorus is heard distantly* could cue the memory of feelings that rise when you listen to music in church. You would expand from what you are hearing (the notes of the music) to the sense memories clustered around the sound. These might include the feel of the high straight back of the pew against your spine, the worn smoothness of the velvet pew cushion, the musty smell of the well-thumbed Bibles, or the sight of the faces in front of you, lifted in expectation to the pulpit.

These sensations—evoked by the high thin voices, and the odd bitter tones of the chorus—might evolve into an image of *serenity*. This somewhat abstract idea is composed of many sensations. You could choose from your memories a church experience that was apt. Not the time you dissolved into giggles when the overweight lady's choir robe split. Maybe the time you sang at your baby sister's communion, or attended a friend's funeral and found solace in the ritual of the ceremony.

If you haven't heard a choir lately, or ever, you can go to a church and listen to such music. How do you feel when you listen? You want to recall that feeling on stage, remembering not just the sound but the sense memories clustered around the sound. These sense memories can be triggered onstage by the sound of the music, just as the *feel* of Madame's fur in *The Maids* might trigger the fantasy images of luxury or class hatred. The theory is that working from the details of your sense memory can lead you reliably to reproduce an emotion and experience onstage. From the cluster of sensations we've labeled a feeling of *serenity* evoked by the music, you would be prompted to a feeling of peace and security:

> *A great chorus is heard distantly, sung by the pilgrims.*

Then, when you are interrupted from your genuine reverie, your reaction will be that of someone genuinely resentful that a non-believer has shattered that peace, profaning what is holy.

Yerma goes toward the cart, and from behind it her husband, Juan, appears.

YERMA Were you there all the time?
JUAN I was.
YERMA Spying?
JUAN Spying.
YERMA And you heard?
JUAN Yes.
YERMA And so? Leave me and go to the singing.

> *She sits on the canvases.*

You will not be pretending to have the shock of being interrupted from reverie, you will be experiencing reverie and such an interruption for real, and in full sight of the audience. You will not be pretending to emote, your emotion will be there, as solid a fact as the floor. This is the appropriate use of sense memory onstage, triggered by the sensations of performing the play.

Substitution

Lorca's text gives many other images to pursue for sense memories: prickly thistles, the shame of name-calling, the little glass of water. But notice that one of the most powerful—a "tiny animal" tormented by small children—is not possible with this approach. You are not a small animal. To gain access to a sense memory, you must substitute an experience of your own. This **substitution** of your own sensations for those in the script is akin to what Polus did with his son's ashes in order to cry as a sister over the death of her brother. Rather than imagining the animal's pain, the Method asks you to substitute your own.

Childhood memories are particularly useful for substitution because the experiences of a child are often dramatic. The American short story writer Carson McCullers said that any artist who survives childhood has enough material to last a lifetime. If you had an older sibling or have ever played in a schoolyard, you almost certainly have had the childhood experience of being bullied. The sensations of that experience are what you can use to put yourself in the place of the animal that Yerma describes. The name-calling that Yerma refers to might remind you of childhood name-calling. You would substitute other insults for the word *barren*. When you hear *barren*, you would respond as if you heard whatever words that initially hurt you.

Substitution can endow even the scenery and properties of a performance with significance. In a performance of *The Maids* there might not be a real sable or a string of baroque pearls onstage, but the actress playing Solange might substitute the image of those things for the rhinestones and beads she handles when she cleans up after Madame.

As with fantasy images, the actors do not need to share the same images for substitutions. These are private and personal. The actress playing Yerma might substitute a childhood memory of *torment*. If you are playing Yerma's husband, Juan, in this scene you could substitute a more innocent childhood experience: *hide and seek*.

Playing Juan, you can't help notice that the actress playing Yerma does not share your images, or join in your game. This is inevitable because while playing the role of Juan, you are preparing for a love scene, while Yerma is preparing for a murder. The frustration of not having a cooperative playmate can be substituted for Juan's frustration with his wife's unhappiness. Again, your emotion will be genuine, not feigned. You will not need to think of ways to express your frustration, you *will be* frustrated that your partner does not respond in the way you want:

YERMA And so? Leave me and go to the singing.

She sits on the canvases.

JUAN It's time I spoke, too.

YERMA Speak!

JUAN And complained.

YERMA About what?

JUAN I have a bitterness in my throat.

YERMA And I in my bones.

JUAN This is the last time I'll put up with your continual lament for dark things, outside of life—for things in the air.

YERMA (*with dramatic surprise*) Outside of life, you say? In the air, you say?

JUAN For things that haven't happened and that neither you nor I can control.

YERMA (*violently*) Go on! Go on!

JUAN For things that don't matter to me. You hear that? That don't matter to me. Now I'm forced to tell you. What matters to me is what I can hold in my hands. What my eyes can see.

Juan's inability to share his wife's image of *childlessness* is an essential aspect of the drama of *Yerma*. For Juan, a child is an encumbrance, and maybe a rival for his wife's affections. For Yerma, a child is the meaning of a woman's life. You may not feel either way about children; performing as Juan or as Yerma you can substitute something you do care about deeply in order to speak with honest passion.

Personalization

According to this way of working, everything you say and do begins with yourself. It is this insistence that the origin of a performance be personal experience—not personal fantasy or mask—that marks the Method. You can start with a substitution (the child for the animal), a sense memory (the friend's funeral), a self-induced sensation (thirst, Dustin Hoffman's sleeplessness), or an experience onstage (*I want to play a love scene but she wants to play a tragedy*), but in any of these ways you begin with *personal images*—not the playwright's, and not the character's.

Personalization is substitution made to correspond with personal history. The question to be answered is not *What is this like?* but rather *How is this like me?* This "finding the character in yourself, rather than yourself in the character" can be developed into an art. In order to create the experience onstage, instead of using fantasies or clichés, an actor can begin with self-examination of experience, and, when life experiences aren't enough to find parallels, explore further with an *improvisation* based on the script.

YERMA (*rising to her knees, desperately*) Yes, yes. That's what I wanted to hear from your lips . . . the truth isn't felt when it's inside us, but how great it is, how it shouts when it comes out and raises its arms! It doesn't matter to him! Now I've heard it!

JUAN (*coming near her*) Tell yourself it had to happen like this. Listen to me.

He embraces her to help her rise.

JUAN Many women would be glad to have your life. Without children life is sweeter. I am happy not having them. It's not your fault.

YERMA Then what did you want with me?

JUAN Yourself!

YERMA (*excitedly*) True! You wanted a home, ease, and a woman. But nothing more. Is what I say true?

JUAN It's true. Like everyone.

YERMA And what about the rest? What about your son?

JUAN (*strongly*) Didn't you hear me say I don't care? Don't ask me any more about it! Do I have to shout in your ear so you'll understand and perhaps live in peace now!

YERMA And you never thought about it, even when you saw I wanted one?

JUAN Never.

Both are on the ground.

The subject of this scene between husband and wife may be a child, but all relationships eventually have moments when partners realize that they are speaking at cross-purposes. Can you recognize yourself in the scene from those times, either in life or onstage, when *you* didn't listen to your partner?

If such a personalization seems remote, a new one can be established in rehearsal. You could do an improvisation, abandoning the script entirely, and natter along until an explosion. It could begin with something as slight as picking up your cues (*Did you hear me?*), or something as gross as suggestively lying down on the ground in expectation that your partner will join you. As the scene continues, the stage direction will gain a personal significance from your previous improvisation.

The forms of improvisation vary from nonsense syllables (a Strasberg technique), to paraphrase (an Adler technique), to wordlessness (a technique used by Stanislavsky in his later years). The aim of the improvisation, however, is to lead the actors back to the text and the demands of the play. When it does not, improvisation is a creative cul de sac—just like any other set of images not translated to the text.

Both are on the ground.

YERMA And I'm not to hope for one?

JUAN No.

YERMA Nor you?

JUAN Nor I. Resign yourself!

YERMA Barren!

JUAN And lie in peace. You and I—happily, peacefully. Embrace me!

He embraces her.

YERMA What are you looking for?

JUAN You. In the moonlight you're beautiful.

YERMA You want me as you sometimes want a pigeon to eat.

An actress playing Yerma based on her experience with sexual aggression might personalize Yerma's horror at her husband's sexual desire. The scene might remind the actor playing Juan of an experience he had seducing an unwilling, naïve girl. However, these direct personalizations may be too close to the playwright's scenario—or too close to the actors—to be understood or applied. For those reasons, or others, it may be more useful to personalize the situation by substituting something else. Personalization and substitution can obviously be combined, and often are.

The idea of personalization is a sound one. Freed from the orthodoxy of the Method, it can be used with fantasy images as well as personal history. As Shylock in *The Merchant of Venice*, Ira Aldridge's fantasy of himself as a persecuted Jew was just as personal an idea as any memory of his childhood as a black man in America.

Emotional narrative

As in work with fantasy images, it's not enough to identify an image from your past. Personal history must be elaborated before it can be applied to the text. Strasberg suggested investigating events from personal history using a technique called **emotional narrative**. The actor begins by departing from the text entirely; not just the words, but the events and the characters the text describes. The actor is instead encouraged to relate, in his own words, an emotionally charged event from his past. Led by the director or acting teacher, the emotional narrative reaches a point where the storyteller identifies emotionally with what he is describing.

Let's say that you are playing Yerma, and this scene has reminded you of the time in your childhood when you were playing with another little girl and the fun turned scary and violent. You came over on a hot Sunday afternoon to play with your friend next door. She took your doll, and you, in a hot rage, choked her until tears came to her eyes. She smashed your doll against the wall. You can still remember that sound. You grabbed your friend by the hair and shoved her head down the way she had shoved your doll. Luckily, you were interrupted by your friend's mother, who sent you home in disgrace. Remembering the sight of your scratched doll still gets you angry, even though it was damaged many years ago. As you tell the story aloud, you find your key to understanding implacable rage. In this way, Yerma's outrage at Juan's sexual overture will be personalized as parallel to your childhood outrage, when your most precious possession was treated lightly and irreverently.

It was not Strasberg's intention to make this exercise a performance technique. Yet, inevitably, that is what happened. The process corresponded to the then-popular psychological idea that uncovering forgotten memory would release a torrent of forgotten feelings. It was irresistible for performers to repeat the process onstage to access and reproduce emotions. But resist you must, because an emotional narrative is a form of expression, not communication. It unblocks a feeling for the person telling the story, *but it ignores the audience.*

As Strasberg led actors through emotional narratives in class, he maintained the professional distance of a therapist assisting a client in the resurrection of some long-repressed trauma. During a performer's recitation of an emotional narrative, the emotional involvement of the listener does not matter to the speaker, who is working on uncovering something inside himself. The excitement of the teacher encouraging the person remembering to go forward is not to be expected from another actor in performance. Nor would it necessarily touch an audience, because, again, this is an exercise performed without concern for the listeners' reaction. You can understand now why this valuable rehearsal technique, which does not need a partner, is an inappropriate performance technique.

> JUAN Kiss me . . . like this.
> YERMA That I'll never do. Never.

> YERMA *gives a shriek and seizes her husband by the throat. He falls backward. She chokes him until he dies.*

The value of the emotional narrative is that it can take a performer to the origin of large emotions and thus provide subject matter for inner images. In the example we've worked with, the strength necessary to choke someone to death is achieved through accessing the primal rage of a child avenging her doll, just as the parched feeling of barrenness was derived from self-induced thirst.

When used purposefully, emotional narrative and sense memories are exercises to gain access to images. Substitution and personalization, when used correctly, are the ways these images are applied to the text.

Justifying: working from the inside out

To avoid the danger that an actor's fascination with private imagery might overwhelm an investigation of the text, images in the Method are never allowed to articulate their own language and forms the way a fantasy image might. Like Stella Adler, Lee Strasberg insisted that images always be yoked to tasks by what is called **justification** (because they justify the onstage behavior). The precedent for this was Stanislavsky.

In the second of the three books issued under his name in English, titled *Building a Character*, Stanislavsky describes Nazvanov—the student actor from Chapter 1 who became comfortable on the stage once he went hunting for a lost nail—now sitting in his dressing room, smearing green and grayish greasepaint onto his face, and staring into a mirror until a character emerges: The Critic. The Critic speaks in a rasping voice utterly unlike the student's own and has motives that are malicious and destructive. He is, if anything, the Spirit of Negativity.

> "[I am] the fault-finding critic who lives inside of Kostya Nazvanov. I live in him in order to interfere with his work. That is my great joy. That is the purpose of my existence." *I was myself amazed at the brazen, unpleasant tone and fixed, cynical, rude stare which accompanied it* (62).

In our vocabulary, we recognize that Stanislavsky was beginning with a fantasy image. The layer of greasepaint was an external mask, which provoked an inner image, The Critic. There is no sense memory, no substitution, no personalization; but notice that the second sentence the Critic speaks is, fortuitously, his super-task!

The technique of working from an external image is *justified* for Stanislavsky by the presence of the task: *to interfere with Kostya's work.* In other writing, Stanislavsky speaks of how, during his career as a professional actor, his inner images energized his tasks when he played Othello and Dr. Stockman in Ibsen's *An Enemy of the People.* Always, Stanislavsky's images are organized around principles of actions and obstacles.

Nowadays, we do not always believe that behavior is motivated, nor do we believe that tasks must inevitably structure performances. Separated from actions and obstacles, personal images still have a legitimate use in performance and rehearsal. If limiting your images to those derived from personal history gets you results, go right ahead and limit yourself. In practice, most actors over time use a combination of both fantasy and experience, and switch back and forth without shame.

To play Yerma, your images can begin with a real sensation of *thirst*, proceed to a sense memory of *church music*, evolve to an elaborate substitution of your *childhood trauma* over a broken doll, and still conclude with a fantasy of a *bird flying with a broken wing*. The sense memory of thirst will set off a task *to gain water*, the *serenity* of church music will have as its justification *to gain inner peace*, the *broken doll* will be one more obstacle to that peace, and the fantasy of the bird will be the fulfillment of a task. The murder will be justified as a way *to fly free of sorrow*, to an oasis of water in the parched Spanish plain.

Even yoked to tasks, the strict separation of fantasy and imagery from personal history is an aesthetic rather than a necessary choice. When the Moscow Art Theater actress Maria Ouspenskaya first settled in New York, one of the things she taught was an animal substitution exercise. Closing an eye to the implications of animal imagery (that some inner images could, indeed, begin with a fantasy experience), Method actors were encouraged to use animals to personalize images. According to the acting teacher Edward Easty, Lee J. Cobb, who played the first Willy Loman in Arthur Miller's *Death of a Salesman*, worked from an inner image of an elephant to give himself the bulk and weariness required by the role (63).

If you substitute the image of *a bird with a broken wing* for Yerma, the image of the pilgrims' choir can alter from human voices to *the sound of the other birds* calling you to join the soaring flock. Translated by the Rosetta Stone of the bird with a broken wing, your thirst will be slaked by flying away from the desert; the music will be the birds' honk or tweet. (Are you a swan? A crow? A nightingale?) The doll fantasy might become *a nest of broken eggs*, and the last image of the scene—when Yerma is discovered with the body of her husband—might become, in your mythology, the time of dawn when birds, even the ones with broken wings, rise over the fields in graceful flight. Yerma's cry will be that of a swan, honking back to the earth she soars away from.

> *The chorus of the pilgrimage begins.*

> YERMA Barren, barren, but sure. Now I really know it for sure. And alone. (*she rises, people begin to gather*) Now I'll sleep without startling myself awake, anxious to see if I feel in my blood another new blood. My body dry forever! What do you want? Don't come near me, because I've killed my son. I myself have killed my son!

> *A group that remains in the background gathers. The chorus of the pilgrimage is heard.* CURTAIN.

If you worked from an image out of your personal experience, you might personalize that cry as the sound you made when your friend's mother found you—an enemy now to your best friend—sitting on the floor with your broken doll. You might hunt down a photograph of yourself at that age, or touch a fragment of a broken doll's head before you rehearse the scene. If the shard of the doll's head is small enough, you might even carry it on to the stage with you—the way Polus carried the ashes of his son.

Let's Review Terms

the Method	a systematic use of personal images
sense memory	the cluster of sensations that when remembered induce an emotion
substitution	your experience parallels the playwright's description
personalization	the use of personal experience
emotional narrative	an event from your past told as a story in order to retrieve a sense memory
justification	the reason something happens onstage

Practical Tips for Working

Learn from Porky Pig

When the inexperienced producers at Warner Brothers first created the cartoon character of Porky Pig, they hired a real stutterer to dub the voice. Think about that. A real stutterer can't control his hesitations; if he could, he wouldn't stutter. A real stutterer can't match up his voice to the film of the cartoon character's stammer. The producers needed to hire an actor who could *simulate* the stutter, and on cue. Just so, when investigating an image in rehearsal, at a certain point you want to be in control of the image enough to match up with the words and action of the text.

Fantasy or images from personal history—you don't want to lose control. You don't want to slam your partner to the floor, you don't want to stick pins in your leg. The point of sense memory is to develop memories and sensations so that you do not have to kill someone when you play a murderer. True, when Alfred Hitchcock filmed *The Birds* he had real birds pecking at the poor actors. This kind of manipulation is available to film directors, but it is not available to stage directors or actors. Even its uses for film acting are limited.

You act AS IF you were reliving the events. You are NOT reliving them; you are remembering them. Stanislavsky put this idea of AS IF at the center of his system. When Stella Adler broke with Strasberg over his insistence on using emotional memory, she went on to stress AS IF in the use of fantasy images. You do not become enraged at your partner, you act AS IF you were enraged. If you really were reliving uncontrollable rage, you'd forget your lines and smash the face of your partner like a doll. This is not being in the moment; this is being an amateur. The ability to control what you do is what makes you a professional.

To give a voice to Porky Pig, Warner Brothers axed the real stutterer and hired Mel Blanc, a man capable of playing a gravel-voiced prospector, a wise-guy rabbit, a lisping millionaire, and, yes, a stammering pig. To do his impersonations, Mr. Blanc did not need to dress up as a pig, nor did he need to regress to a childhood state when he did stutter (since, in fact, he never stuttered as a child). In the same way that Olivier had a basso image for Othello's voice, Mel Blanc had an image of the stutter—a vocal mask. That image gave him Porky's two-steps-forward-one-step-backward character. For other characters, he imitated real people. The lisping Sylvester is a mean-spirited parody of a Warner Brothers producer who actually lisped, but here, too, Mr. Blanc did not haunt the producer's office or analyze him.

Keep a secret

Even more than with a fantasy image, care must be taken when using an image from your past not to discuss it—to keep its potency by using it only in performance. The more explicit you are in performance, the better; describing an image robs significance from the experience of acting it. An image is like the old-fashioned notion of sex or money: people who have it don't talk about it. The more private your image, the more powerful it is to keep it a secret behind the mask of your performance.

Carry a secret

Polus was on to something. Carry an object onto the stage with you that will be your hidden motor for your work. Keep it small; keep it hidden. When Edmund Kean played

Othello, he kept unseen Moroccan coins inside his pocket. When Paul Robeson played Othello, he wore the same earrings Ira Aldridge had worn for the role, given to Robeson by Aldridge's daughter in London—even before Robeson had thought to play the role himself. When Dustin Hoffman played Shylock on Broadway, do you think Olivier's false teeth were tucked somewhere?

Avoid trauma, don't bite off more than you can chew

Dealing with a psychological block in rehearsal is time-consuming and selfish, unless you're playing Hamlet, a character with just such a block, in which case *that* will be your metaphor. It's better to take on something smaller, or just a detail of the larger picture. An image of the last time you saw your former love is more useful than the enormity of the break-up. Similarly, with fantasy you needn't do a full-fledged impersonation, or take the time in rehearsal to perfect imitated mannerisms. Your fantasy image is meant to stir you to work on the script, not to research the exact shade of Jean Harlow's platinum blonde.

Engage, don't enrage, the director

How do you get the director to agree to this kind of work? Directors often have their own ideas of how to waste time in rehearsals. Here's a little secret: except for the very young or very inexperienced, most directors like to steal ideas that are better than their own. They can't help themselves. You as the performer just have to set a little bait for them. You say, "I'm going to try something in rehearsal today. Tell me what you like or don't like about it." This alerts the director to pay attention to what you're doing (as if the six-inch heels and Tina Turner leather miniskirt aren't eye-catching enough). Establish a way for you and your director to communicate ideas on how to translate your images to the text and you will have a partner for your work.

What you're not going to do is say, "I think she's a little bit like Tina Turner. Am I really thinking that?" Or: "I'm going to do a Tina Turner imitation today. Sit back and enjoy it." You don't want to be talking about fantasy images, you want to be acting them out.

What happens when an image goes dry?

The question always comes up: what happens when an image goes dry? After four weeks of performing from the memory of your grandfather, the idea of Gramps isn't doing a thing for you and onstage you're beginning to wonder what you'll have for dinner after the show. Should you switch the image? That's hard to do at first without disrupting the performance. It's helpful to begin with a *detail* from the image, a small close-up: Gramps's walk, his accent, his wink. Remember that externals are steps to get to the internal truth and recall what Gramps means to you as a vital image of, say, piety and fear of God. Try an associated image: Gramps's friend Sam, or the sound of the surf at Gramps's beach house, or the smell of Gramps's cheap cologne called Florida Water.

Any of these might work. Here is where sense memory is useful. Expand the image to all the senses. It's not unlike enlarging the circle of concentration, although in this case the mind extends to the image, not to the circumstances onstage.

Work on images when you're not in a play

The creation of a personal mythology—discovering and investigating your own set of masks—is something that you can do when you're *not* in a play. If there are photographs from your past or in some book that move you, save them. Copy them. If certain music moves you, keep a list. That may sound cold, but it isn't. Take advantage of music's ability to trigger emotions. You'll have your own images that make you cry, or giggle, or sway your hips. There are other possible triggers: scents, certain sounds, certain objects, even mimicry, if the way you mimic combines outer observation and inner imagery.

Over time you will see that you have patterns. You enjoy Barry White, the "Buddha of the Boudoir." *There's* an image to investigate. Pictures of the ocean turn you on. The patterns might give you a clue to what else to investigate: a rhythm and blues concert, a trip to the sea? Maybe there's something about the deep sound of Barry and the deep blue sea that make you think of—your Norwegian grandfather. Vikings might interest you, which might lead you to Cousteau documentaries and a visit to a meat locker to experience extreme cold. Just don't stay too long.

Transforming and type actors: *Touch of Evil*

Does cultivating your own images mean you will begin to play the same kind of character for every role—and end up as a *type actor* who trades on personality? It's not a bad life. Mae West made a very good career for herself playing the same character over and over again, but she herself knew she couldn't stretch it to fill every role that was offered to her. Recognizing her limitations, she turned down such plum roles as Norma Desmond in *Sunset Boulevard*, Mrs. Levi in *Hello, Dolly!* and any number of characters in various Tennessee Williams plays. Does that make her a lesser artist? No, it makes her a specific one—with the self-knowledge of a working professional.

On the other hand, *transforming actors* use their self-knowledge in other ways. Even if you are the kind of actor who changes from role to role, you can only begin with your own personal history and your own fantasies. Stage-trained (and, so far, unwilling to return) Meryl Streep's ability to change herself is the subject of jealous parody. She is famous for her vocal masks, but she also disguises herself with wigs, make-up, and costumes. Her range has limits, but she has no identifiable "type."

Robert De Niro is an actor who often transforms *within* type—gaining weight to play a boxer in *Raging Bull*, learning to play the saxophone for the musical *New York, New York* (1977)—but he still keeps within a range of the masks he has discovered inside himself, made up of controlled rage and outbursts of violence. In film, De Niro's passion for experiencing the life of someone other than himself led him to insist, very early in his career, that he lie in a grave when the character he was playing was dead. De Niro hoped the camera would record the dirt being shoveled over him, covering his face. Shelley Winters, who was playing his mother, was graveside, bawling hysterically (intent on an emotional memory?). When she realized it was De Niro and not a dummy in the grave, she stopped the scene, genuinely worried for De Niro's safety (64).

There's nothing wrong with being a personality actor if you can manipulate that personality to the role. To create a myth of yourself and then play it onstage successfully requires artistry—and hard work. Sometimes the mask can explain and amplify the role—think of Whoopi Goldberg and Robin Williams in their film roles. Sometimes a mask can obliterate the role—look at the grossly overweight Marlon Brando in Francis Ford Coppola's film *Apocalypse Now* (1979). Coppola, a film director who loves actors, tried to make a metaphor between the self-indulgence of Brando and the decadence of the role he was playing. But Brando was no longer self-aware enough to make it work.

Don't complain that type-acting is by definition narcissistic and unrelated to acting as the art of human relationships. Yes, many performers stop at this step. They reach a plateau where they create a voice and an image for themselves, and then apply them as a mask to whatever role they happen to be doing. The rest of the actors can drop dead behind them and they wouldn't know until they realized there's no one to give them their cue. If you plan to be a legend and an icon, try stretching your talent—and perhaps your acclaim—and have your mask take the story and the other actors into account.

Let's look at some transforming and type actors in the 1958 film *Touch of Evil*, directed by Orson Welles. It's a black-and-white B-movie made relatively quickly (forty-two days) and cheaply (for less than $900,000). The film is most famous for its opening sequence, an unbroken three-minute tracking shot that follows a ticking bomb across the Mexican border and into a seedy southwestern town. The story of the film is the investigation of the explosion. Orson Welles himself acted the role of a corrupt border town sheriff.

Welles was trying to work on time and on budget. His previous inability to do so had led to his banishment from the studio system; he had not directed a Hollywood film for ten years before *Touch of Evil*. Taking advantage of the B-movie limitations, Welles created a spiky, unsettling visual style and made highly dramatic use of sound. During production he was busy fighting with his producers; thus preoccupied, he left his actors alone to do what each did best. They were a colorful collection of individuals, and they each did their best differently.

For purposes of comparing performance techniques, this film is ideal, practically a documentary. In 111 minutes you get to watch a practiced *transforming actor* (Welles), a shameless *type actor* (Marlene Dietrich), eager *Method actors* (Dennis Weaver, et al.), and cliché-spinning *professionals*, 1950s vintage (Charlton Heston and Janet Leigh).

The most compelling is Welles, who creates a complex portrait of a brutal and greedy tyrant. More than a touch of evil, he's a bloated bag of lies. In all his roles, onstage or on screen, Welles used fantasy images to transform himself. Here, in good health at the age of forty-two, he put on a false nose, padded himself to grossness, and flattened his accent to gravel. His unflattering make-up gave him the look of a dried-up drunk studded with gin blossoms. From entrance to exit there is nothing of Orson Welles to be seen; he is submerged in the character. The role itself is a collection of masks: *crusty professional, fallen alcoholic, cunning manipulator, desperate liar, corrupt policeman*. For all the exciting camera work, the dramatic action of *Touch of Evil* is in Welles's performance as he changes from one mask to another. The uncovering of his corruption and his loss of face are moving and complex. As the dying sheriff lies on his back panting out his life, we mourn for him.

Marlene Dietrich plays his old Mexican flame; or rather, she plays Marlene Dietrich. Oh, the character has another name—"Tanya" (not very Mexican)—but it's the same Dietrich persona from many other films, other masks of herself strung together: the *jaded tart* of a frontier bordello (*Destry Rides Again*), combined with an *enervated siren* (*The Blue Angel*), and a *world-weary fortuneteller* (*Ramona*). Dietrich's German accent stays marvelously intact in Mexico, and she is accompanied just as miraculously by a player piano that cranks out something very much like her Berlin signature song, "Lili Marleen." As Tanya, Dietrich shamelessly plays to type, and though her mannerisms are appropriate for the role, they create no illusion of another person.

Besides type and transforming actors, *Touch of Evil* is chockablock with other 1950s acting styles. Charlton Heston and Janet Leigh play naïve Americans lost south of the border. Heston plays a Mexican district attorney who speaks accent-free English—and whose make-up leaves him looking as if he'd been dipped in milk chocolate. Other than the greasepaint, Heston makes no attempt to transform to Hispanic; even his Spanish has an American accent. But never mind, he's good at what he does, playing a cliché image of the period: the 1950s *leading man of integrity*.

Janet Leigh, playing his wife, acts a 1950s *innocent blonde leading lady* (don't tell Dietrich), lost in a (Communist-infiltrated?) third world of not-very-nice people. The innocent-blonde and man-of-integrity roles are built of images that fulfil the B-movie and *film noir* stereotypes. The cornball dialogue sounds genuine coming out of their mouths, in a way it wouldn't from "believable" characters.

Touch of Evil also boasts a collection of young stylish actors, among them a motorcycle gang led by Mercedes McCambridge as a leather-jacketed female version of the motorcycle rebels played by more famous Method men like Brando and James Dean. Dennis Weaver plays a young "eccentric" motel owner, improvising and pausing—and grunting, giggling, and twitching. The would-be Method-acting gang's wide-eyed portrayal of drug-induced euphoria is as entertaining as Janet Leigh's wide-eyed stupefaction at meeting impolite people, although certainly not as fascinating as when Dietrich gives the fat old sheriff a languorous glad-eye. Welles squints a lot in his shots; so convincingly that you'd swear it's a real rogue sheriff shoved in front of the camera. Of course, it isn't. Welles had been just as convincing the year before, on Broadway as King Lear.

And look who is playing the blustering Mexican gangster "Uncle Joe." It's Akim Tamiroff, an actor from Stanislavsky's Moscow Art Theater. What was his task? To get a job. Was his Armenian accent an obstacle? Not in this case: it was an opportunity to substitute the rolled *rrrr*s of Russia for those of a Spanish vocal mask.

Collage

When actors place image on image, a useful analogy for performing is the art of *collage*. In creating a collage, an artist takes already-formed objects—or already-formed pictures—from other sources and places them together in order to produce an effect, an image, greater than the sum of the parts. The word *collage* was coined to describe the work of a group of artists called the *Dadaists*, whose response to the First World War was to create art as an illogical combination of the wreckage of civilization. The name *Dada* was chosen at random, and appealed to the group because it had no meaning. The Dadaists assembled theater events, too—what we now call *performance art*—without plot, without logic, and without characters. Words, if used at all, were part of an assemblage of images.

The word "collage" could be used especially to describe the work of Max Ernst, an older German member of the group, whose fertile imagination invented new techniques of assemblage and the creation of images.* Among many other ways of arriving at a new image,† Ernst cut out images from catalogs, engravings, newspaper advertising, and book illustrations and arranged them together in startling and evocative ways. In a collage by Ernst called *Quietude*, a fashionably dressed man leans back in an upholstered armchair, bobbing on the surface of stormy waves. A woman's left arm and talon-like hand lift up from a ripple below him. The man's legs cross nonchalantly at the ankles and stretch above the water. Behind him, a tower erupts, shrouded in a column of water that blows off into a spray. In the black and white print, the spray looks like leaves, or flames, or vapor. The man's eyes are closed. Is he oblivious to what is around him? Is he thinking of all these things? What is the curious bent rod to the right of the armchair, with what looks like an eye on its handle? The chair is from an advertisement, the sea is from another source, probably an engraving or a book illustration. Where do the woman's arm and the mysterious rod come from? As with an actor's combination of images, the impact of a collage is greater than the sum of its individual parts.

Ernst resisted creating a codified set of images, and enjoyed the mystery and illogic of his connections. Other collage artists, though, created entire and consistent vocabularies of images, with their own Rosetta Stones of meaning. One of the greatest artists with a vocabulary of images was the New York sculptor Joseph Cornell. Cornell assembled objects inside boxes: glass shards on blue velvet, an antique doll crushed behind a curtain of twigs, a parrot against a whitewashed wall or above a coil of wire, an owl in a dirt-encrusted box. Like an actor investigating his own mythology, Cornell built *systems of associations*. Owls, connected to darkness, were the opposite of parrots, which were connected to the sun. A viewer need not share these particular associations. The art objects are evocative for each viewer's dark forest (a child lost in the woods), bright hopes (a parrot chattering in the sun), or shattered dreams (cracked glass).

In the same way, an actor assembles images—fantasies or personal experiences—without explanation. Roles, once assembled, are compositions that have their own meanings. Remember our collage for *Yerma*? It was built up of a free mix of personal and fantasy images:

---

*Ernst once staged a Dada event in a men's room.

†In 1941, at a bookshop in New York City, Ernst held an exhibition and displayed a new technique: a canister on a string with a hole punched in the bottom. Paint was poured in and the dripping canister swung above a canvas. Jackson Pollock, who was watching, was so taken with the notion of drip painting that Ernst created a painting named for Pollock, *Young Man Intrigued by the Flight of a Non-Euclidean Fly*. The painting was originally named *Abstract Art, Concrete Art* a few years before the "Abstract" painters called themselves by this title.

- great thirst
- a gospel choir
- childhood name-calling
- marital nagging
- sexual aggression
- a smashed doll's head
- attacking a friend in a childish rage
- a bird with a broken wing
- a nest of broken eggs
- a flying swan
- a piece of eggshell

The Chart

Let's return to the chart. There are still some categories to fill in for *Building Images.*

- **Illusion of character.** Collecting a *string of masks* creates the illusion of character for an actor building a role with images.
- **Dramatic action.** Dramatic action happens with the *change from one mask to another.*
- **Unifying image.** The unifying image is a *collage,* where images are placed together to make evocative combinations.
- **Suitable playwrights.** Plays that include a playwright's strong imagery are best acted when an actor's imagery is equally strong. The fantasy images of *Strindberg, Genet, Pirandello,* and *Samuel Beckett* need to be translated into a performer's own, as do the heightened psychological images of *Tennessee Williams, Eugene O'Neill,* and *Federico García Lorca.*

Responsibility—Not Just Response—to the Words of the Play

In the television series *Saturday Night Live,* the sadly short-lived comedienne Gilda Radner played a character who was a television commentator named Emily Litella. This opinionated older lady would offer stinging responses to the problems of the day. "What's all this fuss I keep hearing about violins on television?" she would ask provocatively. Or: "What's all this fuss about Soviet Jewelry?" Given a topic, Emily would rattle on: "Now, if they only showed violins after ten o'clock at night the little babies would all be asleep and they wouldn't learn any music appreciation . . . I say there should be more violins on television and less game shows! It's terrible . . ." until someone would point out that the issue was *violence* on television, not *violins.* Soviet *Jewry,* not Soviet *Jewelry.* Emily would invariably end her commentary with an abrupt: "Never mind!"

As an actor, you're meant to have a responsibility, not just a response, to the words of the play. No matter how deeply you personalize your images, if you don't bother to understand what you are saying, your worked-up feelings are as pointless as Emily Litella's.

BUILDING IMAGES

On the simplest level, as an actor you're responsible for knowing your lines and not rewriting them because you can't remember them. On the next level, you're responsible for understanding what the words you say and listen to mean. There is no excuse for bewildering the audience because you yourself are confused. Emily had plenty of images to use when she defended "violins on television." The final responsibility, once you do understand what you are saying, is to communicate that understanding to an audience while you're performing.

When you work from images, the responsibility of communicating your ideas involves some choices about style; in other words, the images of the production. Before those choices can be made, when different actors with strong individual images get together in rehearsals, it's often a shock: the *Bride of Frankenstein* strides alongside somebody's *Aunt Bessie* and meets up with—*Barry White*.

If you and the director like the theatricality of dueling images placed together, you can create a collage-like performance style for the production of the play. The Wooster Group and the American director Richard Schechner do just that, freely combining images to create theatrical montages of style. It is a delicate balancing act between two aspects of a production, aspects well described by the French playwright Jean Cocteau in a preface to his scenario for a 1936 dance-drama called *The Eiffel Tower Wedding*:

> The action of my piece is pictorial, though the text itself is not. The fact is that I am trying to substitute a "theater poetry" for the usual "poetry in the theater." "Poetry in the theater" is a delicate lace, invisible at any considerable distance. "Theater poetry" should be a coarse lace, a lace of rigging, a ship upon the sea. *Wedding Party* can be as terrifying as a drop of poetry under the microscope. The scenes fit together like the words of a poem (65).

When a performer's images are most effective, they translate the "poetry in the theater" to "theater poetry." Approaching a script, that is your responsibility: to transform the text into a performance.

The danger is that the theater poetry will out-shout the poetry in the theater and that the text will be lost, or adjusted to fit the dramatic action defined by the switch of masks. Badly done, this is not so much translation as adaptation, and frequently involves cuts in the text, transpositions, and additional writing.

The conventional technique is to slowly, slowly translate the specifics of your images into the words of the play, and in doing so, create a consistent world for the production of the play. If the image for Hedda Gabler is a *wolf locked in a cage*, in the world of Victorian Norway the bars of the cage transform into the laces of a corset. If you're setting *In the Jungle of Cities* in Chicago, you'll want more than a vocal mask, you'll want an accurate Chicago accent. Your image for Madame in *The Maids* might be Jean Harlow, but in the world of a Parisian flat there will be a mirror to stare at instead of a movie camera. Yerma's sexual frustration will be defined by the standards of ultra-Catholic southern Spain; it wouldn't be compared to thirst, but to the unnatural cravings of a dipsomaniac. More ways to inhabit the world of the play? For that you need a *world of the play analysis*, which is, fortunately, the subject of the next chapter.